A SOLDIER & his REDHEAD

FALLING STARS FROM WWII

TO

F.A.D.

A Soldier & His Redhead
Copyright © 2020
By Jesse LaVerd Dobson

Dedicated to Flora Adams Dobson
Printed in the United States of America

Design by Lisa Dobson Potter
Preface by Loralie Dobson Matsuda
Edited by Lisa Dobson Potter and Loralie Dobson Matsuda

Printed in the United States of America

Published by Dobson Family Publications
lisapottersemail@gmail.com

First edition
ISBN: 9798633163872

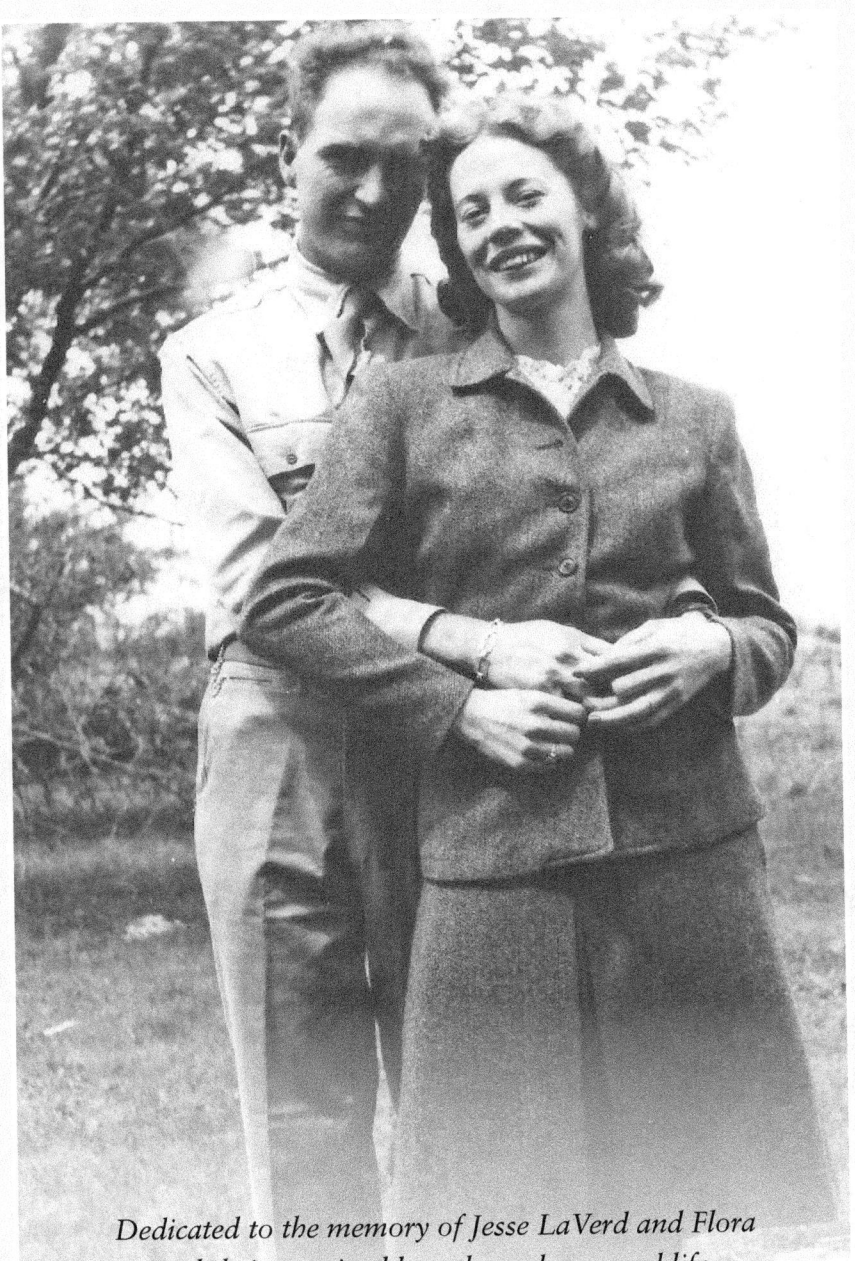

Dedicated to the memory of Jesse LaVerd and Flora
and their entwined love through war and life.
★

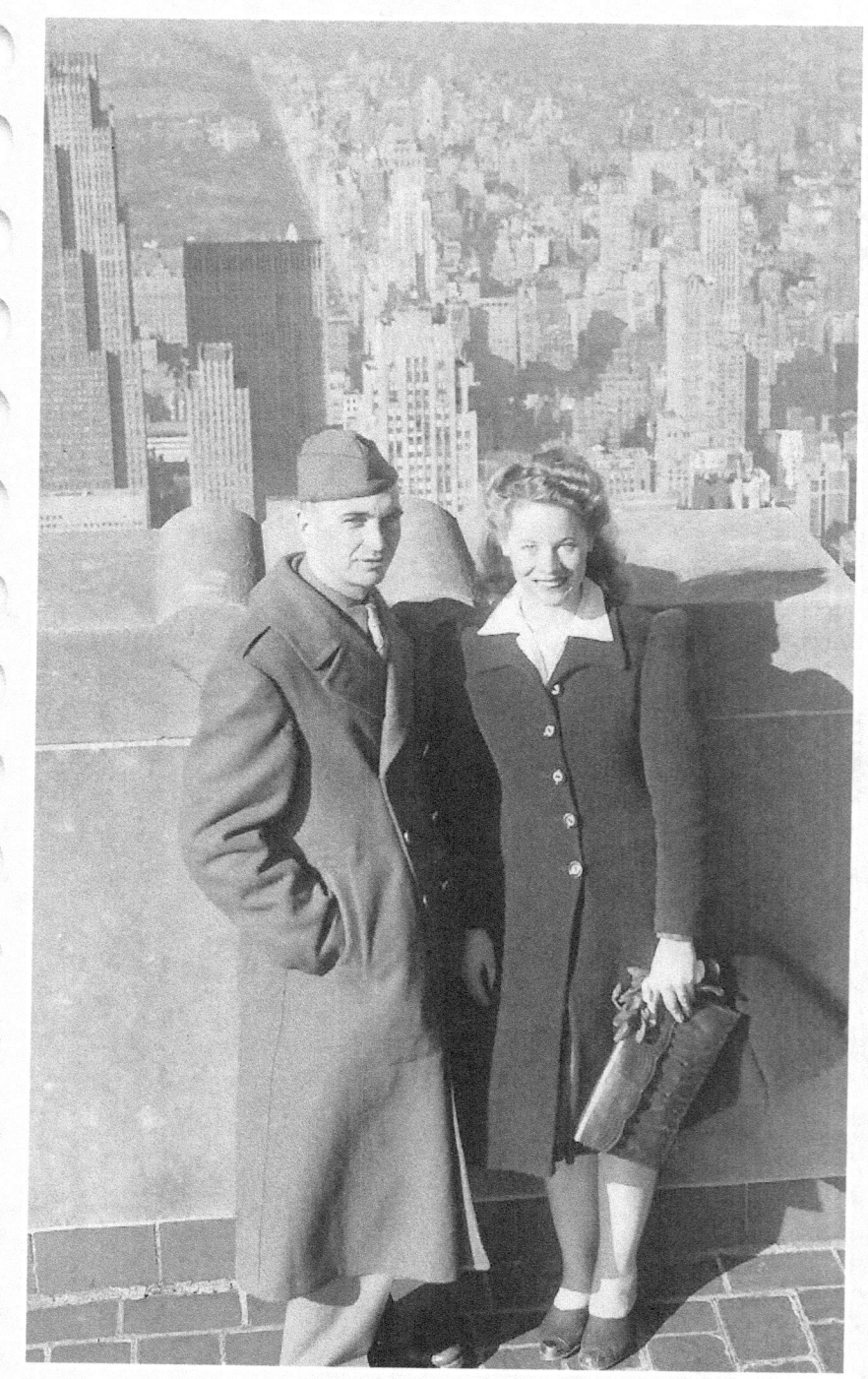

Our Soldier, Jesse LaVerd Dobson, was drafted into service on April 21, 1941. He first served stateside, then in North Africa and Italy during World War II.

His Redhead, Flora Adams, married him on December 9, 1942—two days after the bombing of Pearl Harbor.

His Redhead spent months following her Soldier around on Greyhound buses from one base to another, sometimes falling asleep on the long back seat as the bus rumbled through the night. All this so they could spend precious bits of time together before his unit was shipped overseas.

While apart, our Soldier kept their love shining bright sending letters home including his own heart-felt poetry. His Redhead sent back a few of her own. Our Soldier put them all in a red hand-tooled leather booklet as pictured on this cover—which he illustrated with drawings of falling stars that arched over their marriage for 42 years.

J. LaVerd Dobson
Italia MCMXXXXIV

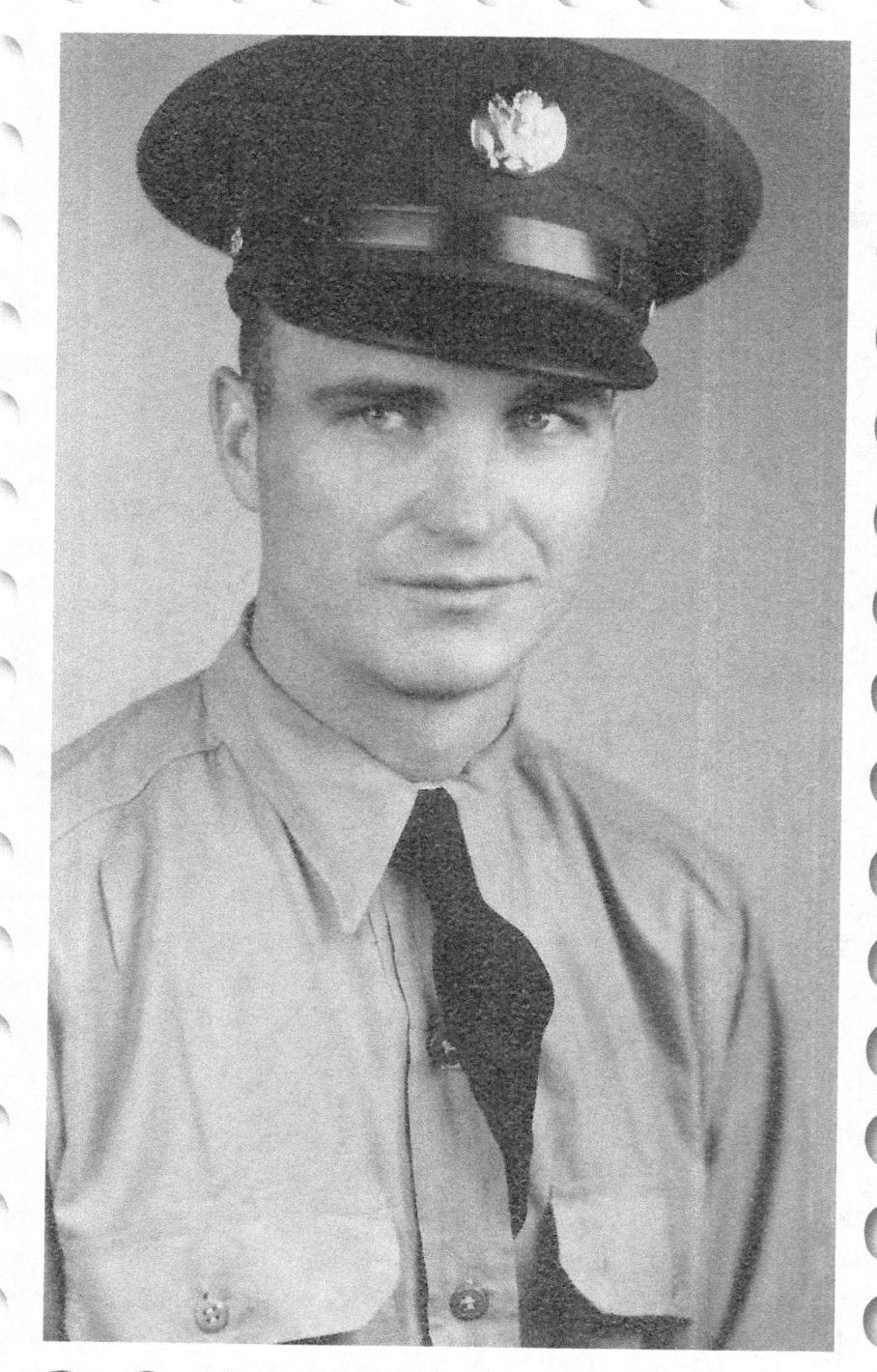

THE SOLDIER & HIS REDHEAD

Italy

June 1944

My Dearest One,

So many nites I've tried—then tried again to write one poem for this most important page of all. Many times I've wondered why these same thots must remain unsaid and unexpressed of this beautiful ideal, this tantalizing and all-elusive something that is you!

But every definition, word or thot expressed by form is limiting. No matter how well chosen or arranged, words will reduce these thoughts to finite terms. So I leave this page with no mischoice of words nor slip of pen, no imperfectly expressed thots or faults that neither mar nor limit dreams and love.

And now—goodbye until another day. And then together you and I may dream our life and love.

May yours be Peace Profound.

LaVerd

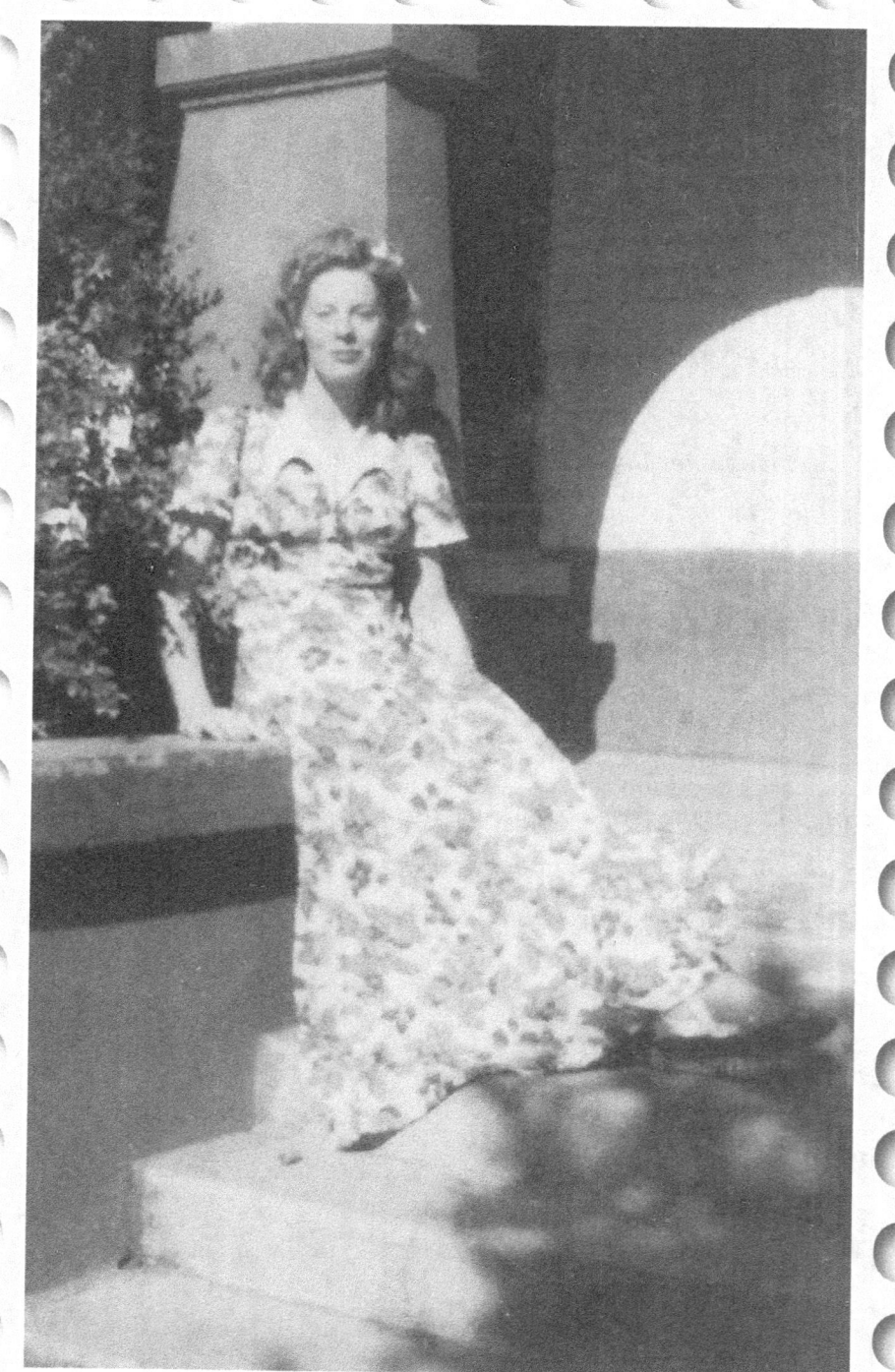

Falling Stars

So many stars in silver trails
Were falling from on high
That soon it seemed, no shining stars
Would be left in the sky.

I wondered if the dying stars
Would fall to earth below—
Or where their fiery trails would lead,
And where does stardust blow?

Of falling stars in velvet blue
I dream when day is done:
Each falling star becomes my dream
Unfolding one by one.

Jesse LaVerd
North Africa, 1943

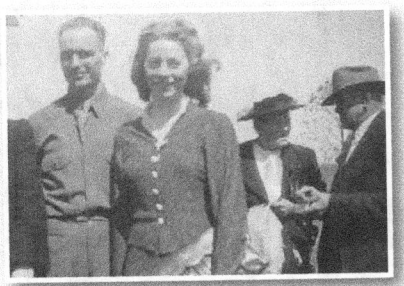

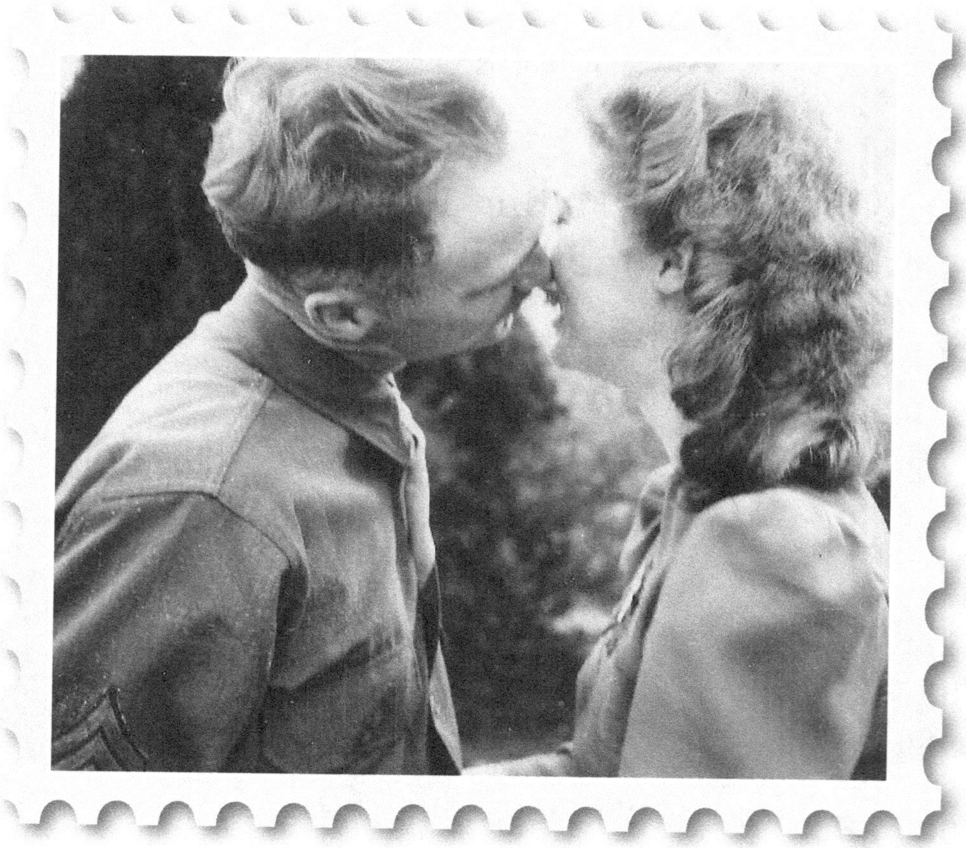

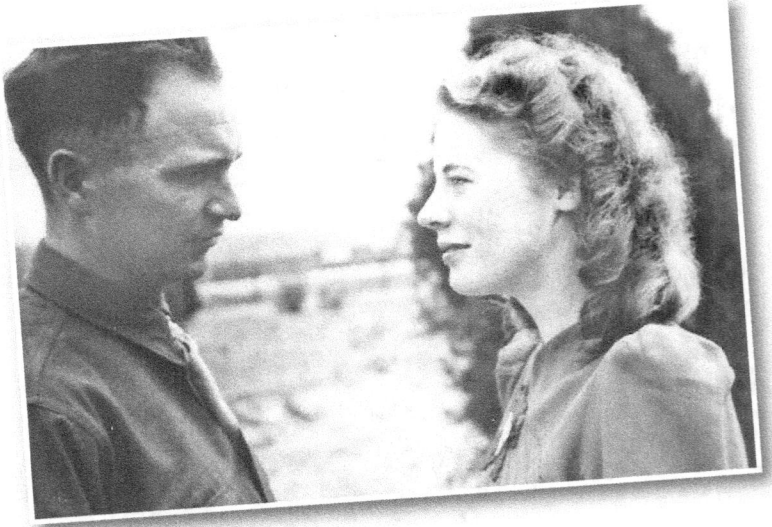

All the Winds

Thruout these hours my soul feeds
deeper flames
How fitting then—this cast-off
garment too
Will be consumed, then flung to
all the winds
That it may be a part of flowers,
trees and rain—
I shall not die.

Jesse LaVerd

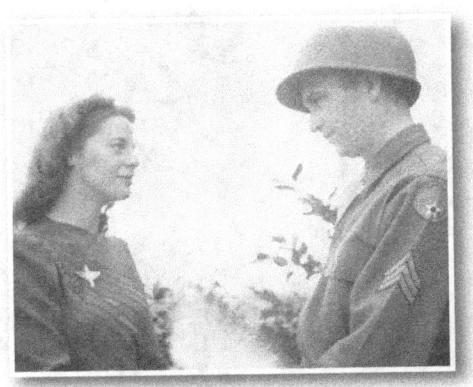

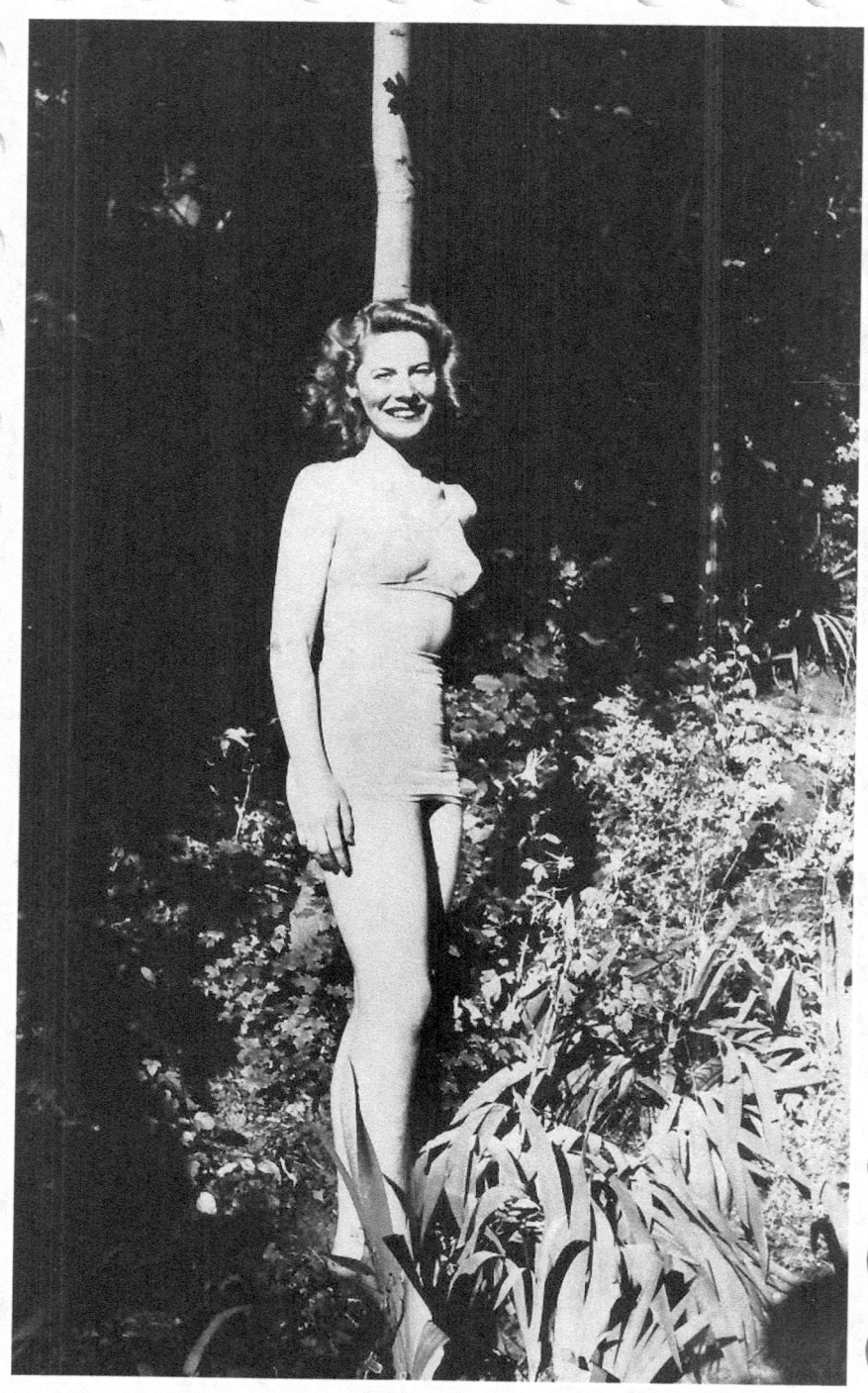

THE SOLDIER & HIS REDHEAD

Poem XVI

Paling star
How beautiful you were,
How bright your radiance
And now so pale of hue.

With luster fading to the day
These moments you depart—
How is it you remain
So constant and untroubled?

Perhaps—could this be so!
You too can know
Another nite descends
And that again your ray serene
Will shine upon the world:

Each nite becomes your day.
Please tell me, Paling Star,
Is this your secret? To know
That you will shine again
As bright as now?

Continues

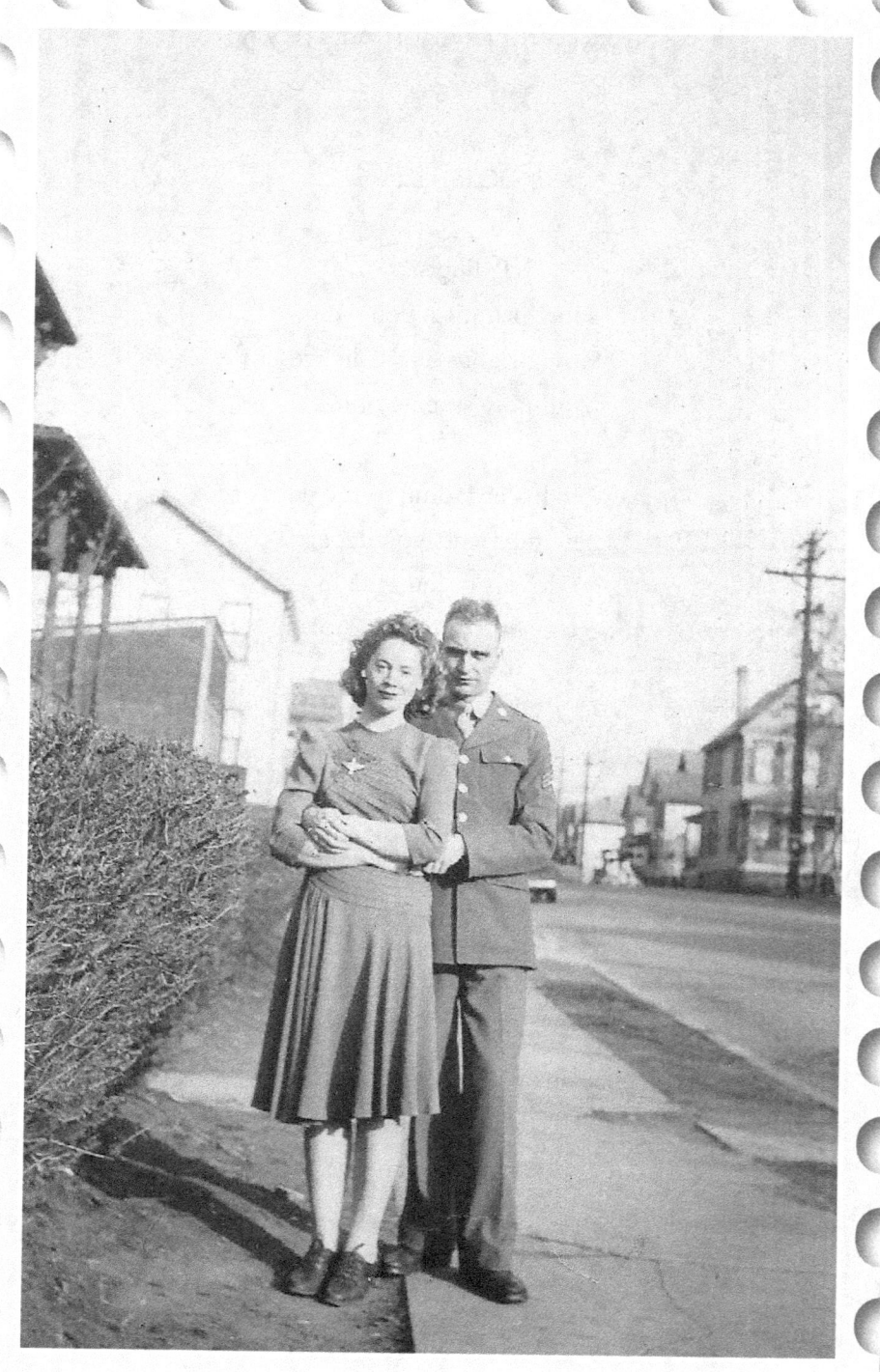

I wonder, Paling Star, if when my day is fading
I too may look upon the world
With gaze serene
And know that I—as you—
Will live again tomorrow.

Jesse LaVerd
North Africa, August 1944

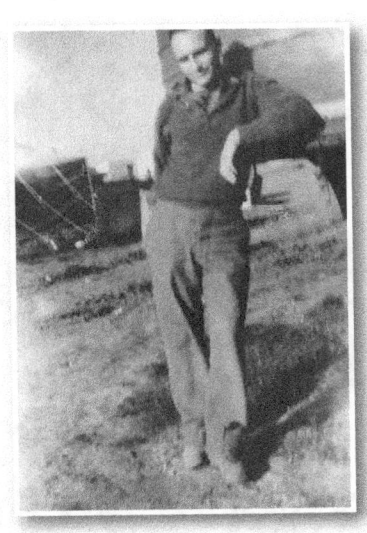

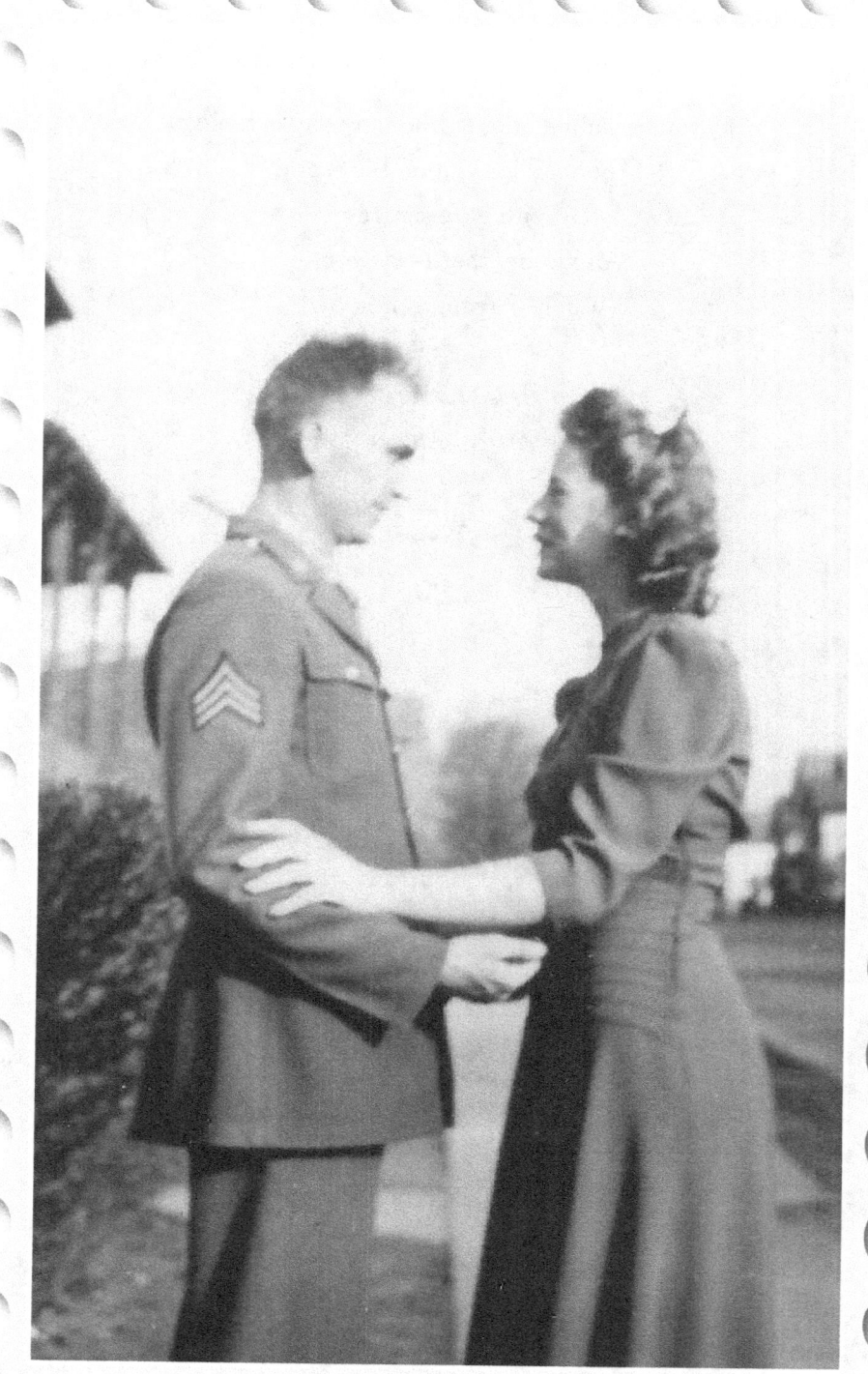

THE SOLDIER & HIS REDHEAD

Our Star

I have seen our star
White and glowing
Shimmering in the desert nite,
Or paled by moonbeams
Then lost among the clouds.
I have watched our star
Blue-white, shining down
Upon this sand and sea
Bidding radiance to be subdued
When vanishing in water,
Dropping from the sky.
I have sent our star
A message long and sweet,
A song, a word of love, a hope, an inspiration
All this, and more—ah,
So much more!—have I sent
Upward and skyward to our star
To give you dreams.
I have seen our star
White and glowing, and with its stardust
I have sent my love to you.

Jesse LaVerd
North Africa, August 1944

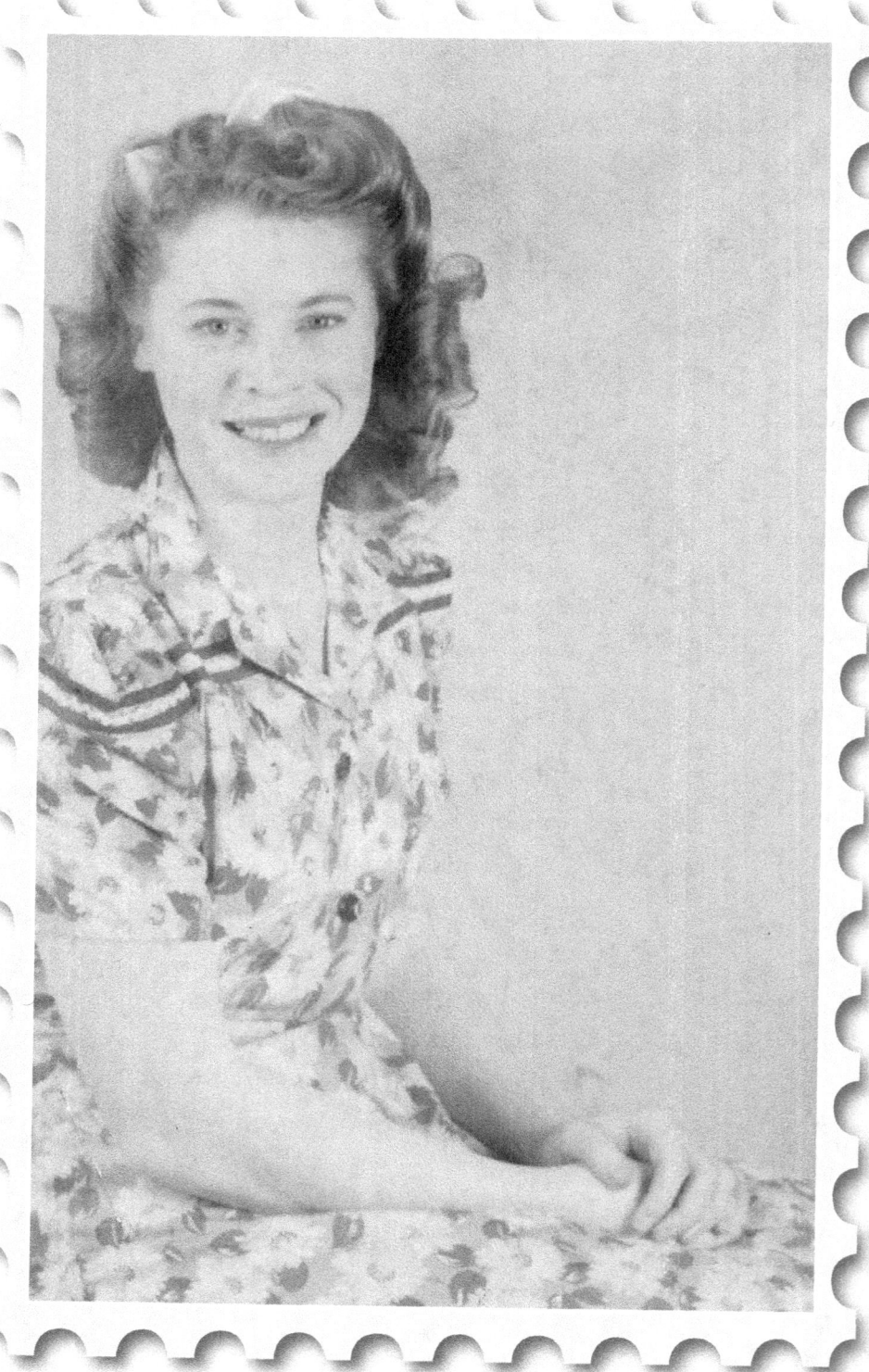

I Dream of You

I dream of you—
See your face, touch your hand.
And live again those hallowed memories.
I speak to you—
And in the silences of nite
I hear your voice, sweet and calling.
I long for you—
And fancy brings you near,
I know again the ecstacy of you.
I dream of you—
Those days and hours
Shrouded by memory, made scared by tears,
Those dreams of you—
And dreams of coming years.

Jesse LaVerd

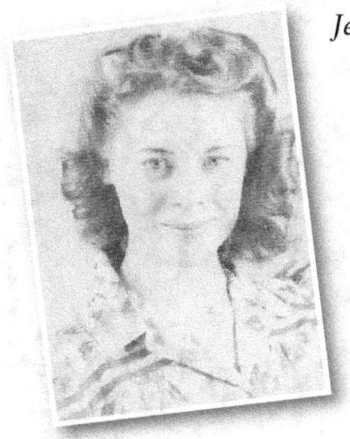

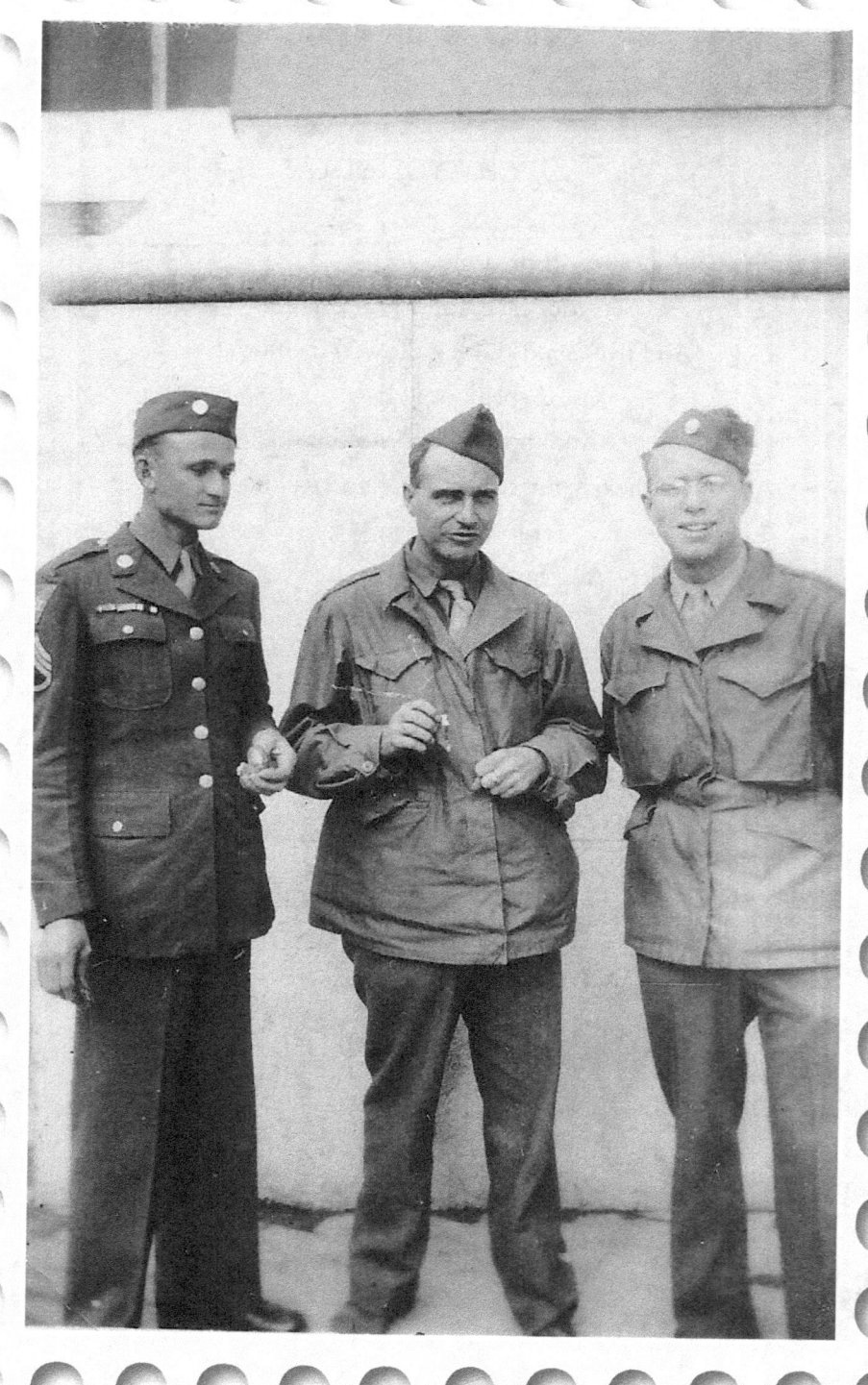

Memorabilia

As blue horizons run the world
These moments days and years
Form the fading yesterdays:
Beautiful and true
Always distant, vague
Unreached
But always there.

Jesse LaVerd

★

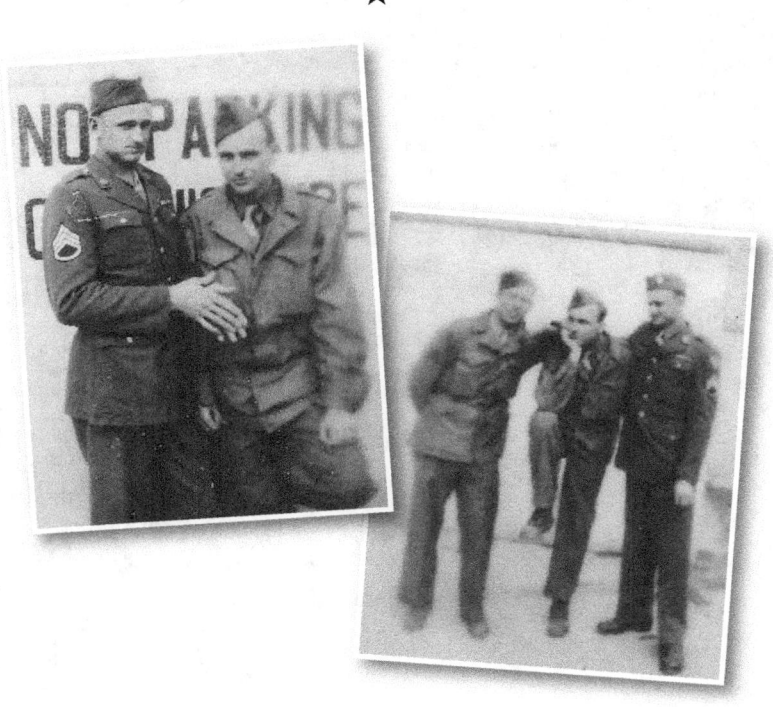

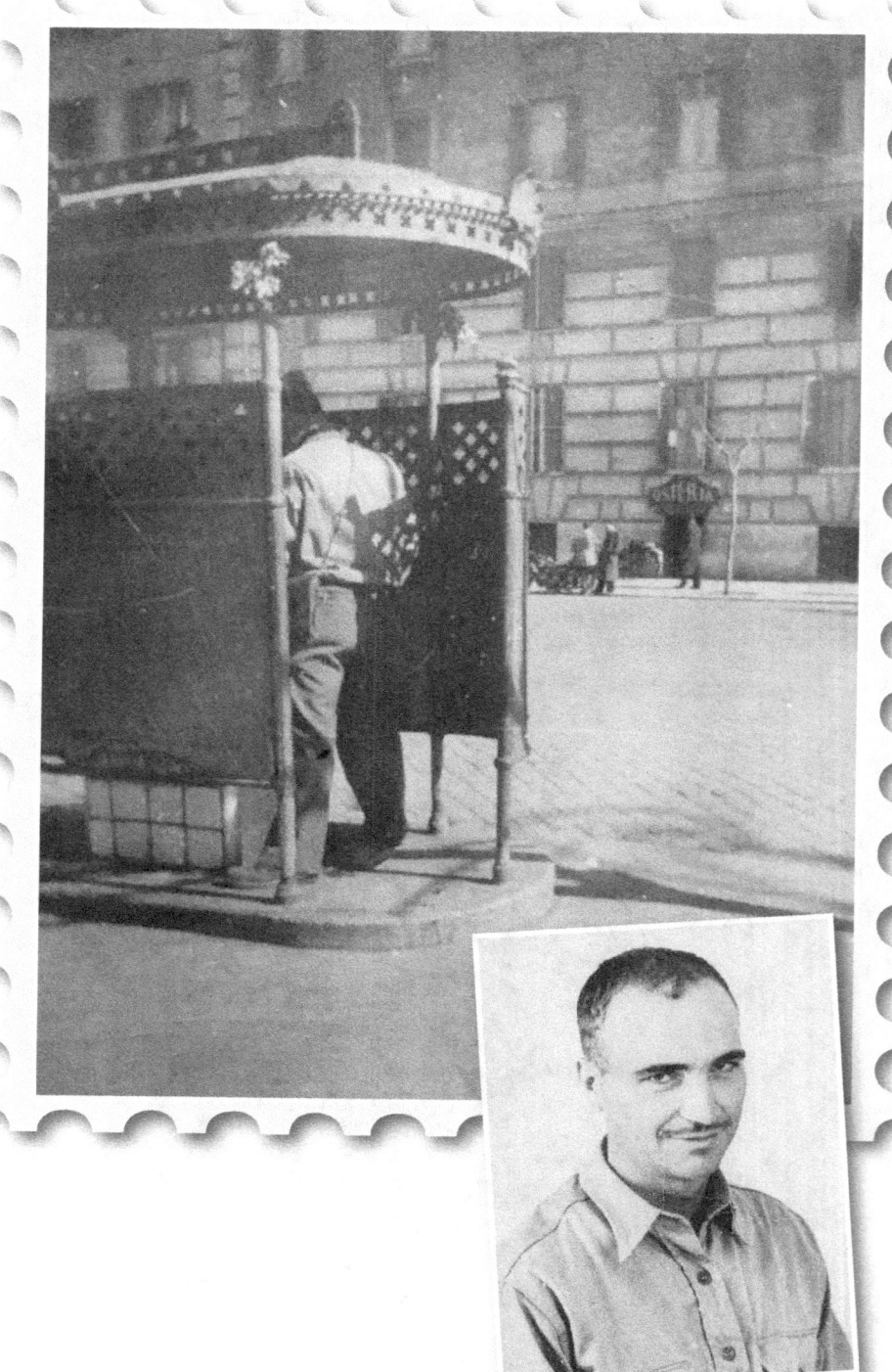

From a Soldier

Thoughts, orders, you—all day,
And each struggling for recognition
Within my mind, my thoughts,
The letters, orders, schedules,
You—all clamoring within my mind.

"Pursuant to authority—"(I love you!)
"You will return this station ..."
(I miss you terribly; wish you were here!)
"Schedule for Wednesday ..."
(Remember our night at the Metropolitan?)

"This letter please, original, four carbons ..."
(I wrote you yesterday—and did you read ..."
"Hurry! Take this to Headquarters ..."
(We were almost afraid—the ceremony ..."

Continues

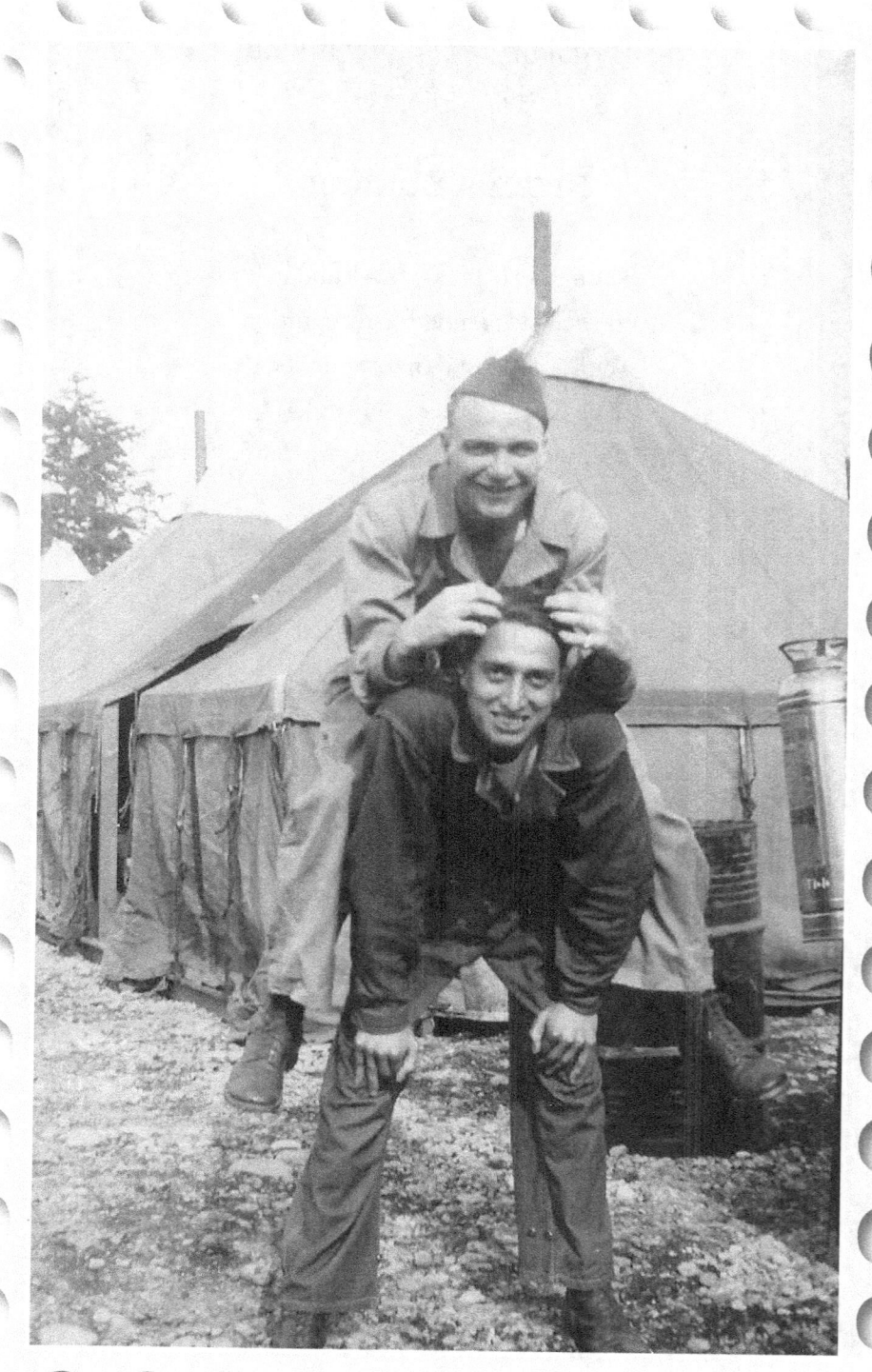

"How many hours flown yesterday?"
(At the USO —you were so sweet ....
I was afraid—leaving you ...)
"This report to be in by ten o'clock ..."

And thus it goes; moments merge into hours,
And hours to weeks, and, perhaps, weeks
To years, before that time—
With always letters, orders, you,
Schedules, you, you, you—!
And time must go on.

Jesse LaVerd
Italia, 1944

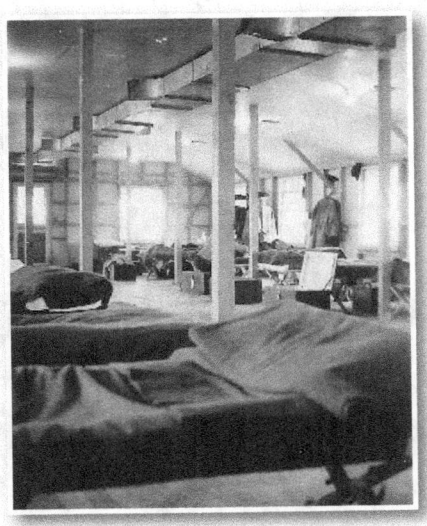

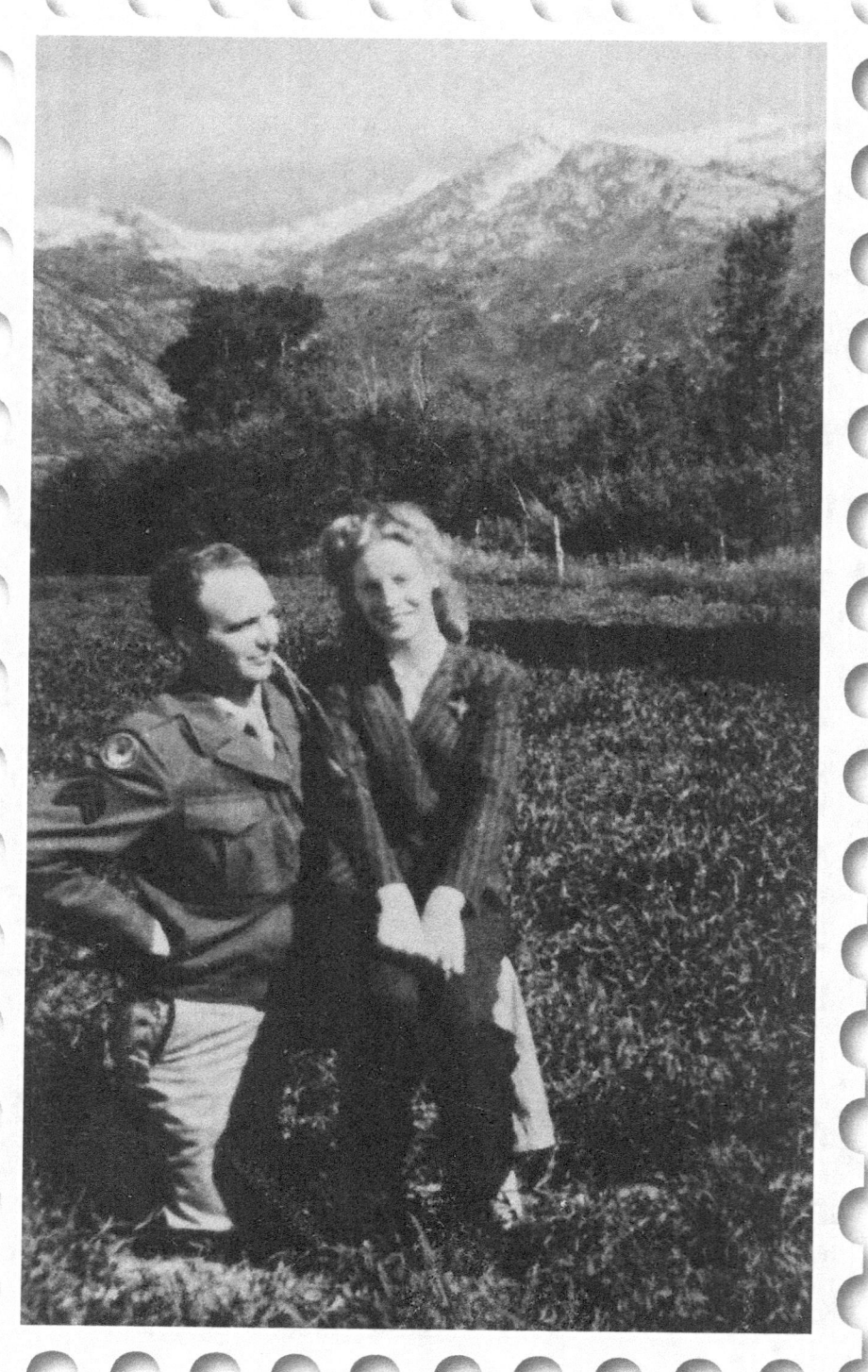

After Rain

The storm brot rain and wind,
and left a gloom
Which seeped around my heart
for company.

Then walking thru the grass and
water by the road,
I found these flowers—blooming
Among the weeds and rain.

I picked them carefully
(These blossoms touched with shades of sky)
And breathed into their fragileness
My hopes, my dreams, my prayers,
My love to you, all breathed into
These flowers of yesterday
I found that morning
After rain.

Jesse LaVerd

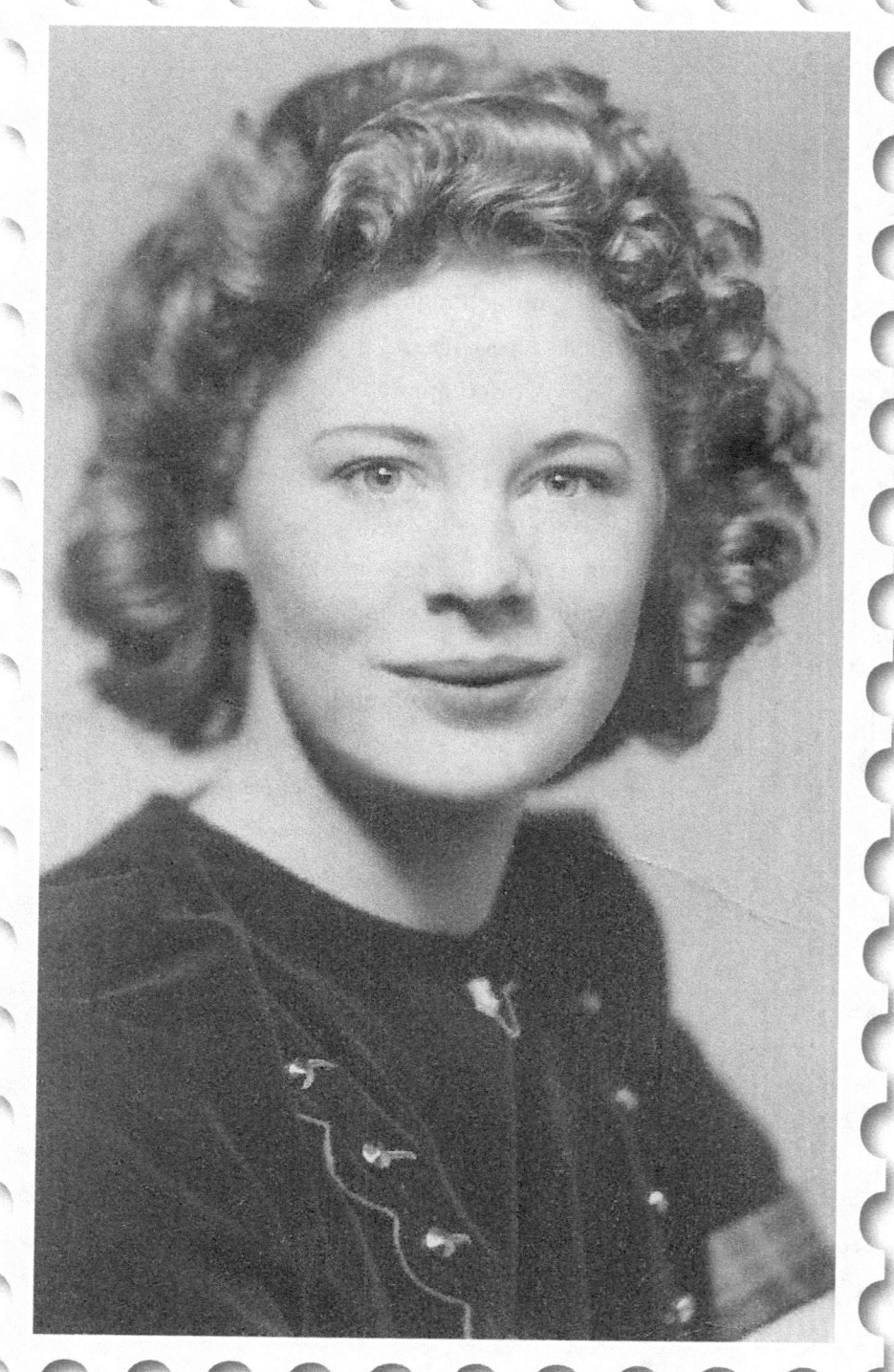

Once Again

Packed in that handsome old hall hushed
and waiting
Their features just barely in view,
The famed names and faces from those
"far off places"
Linked us with the old and the new;
On that last Sabbath Day we found spring,
You and I,
And then once again said good bye.

Flora, 1943

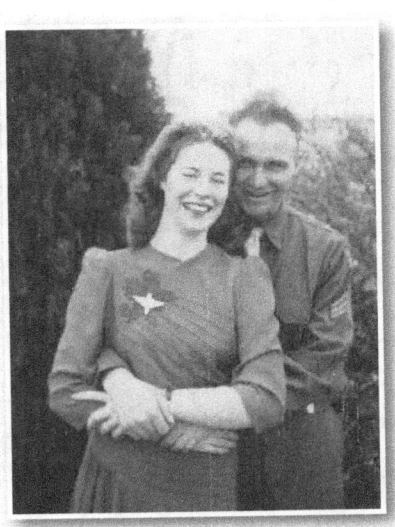

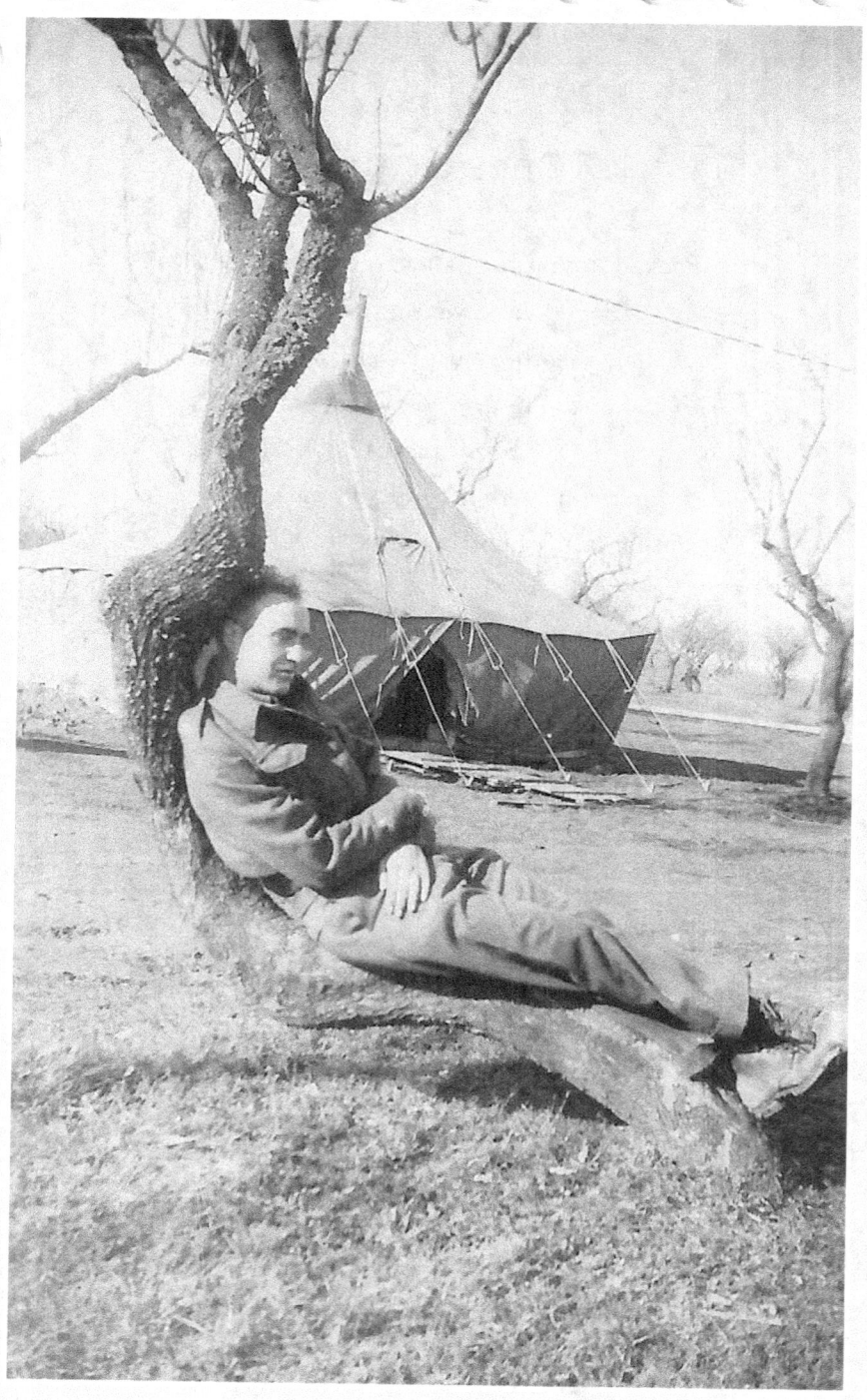

THE SOLDIER & HIS REDHEAD

Another Spring
(A Soldier Confined to Barracks)

They say that spring has come—
This? No green, no flowers?
Only wind and mud,
trees yet shivering in nakedness;
Only multi-colored buildings
Beyond confines of barrack doors—
Is this another spring?

Continues

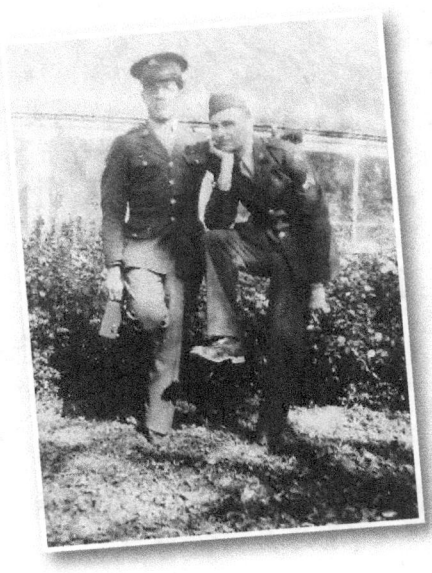

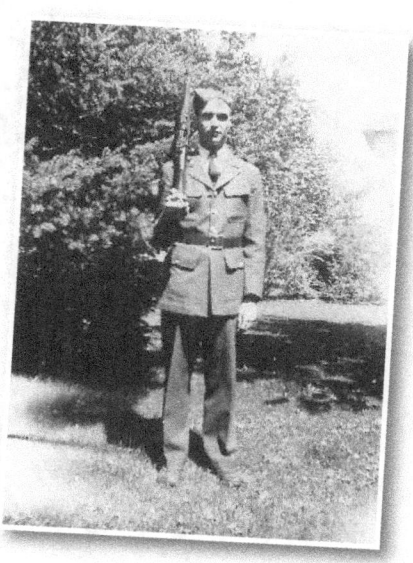

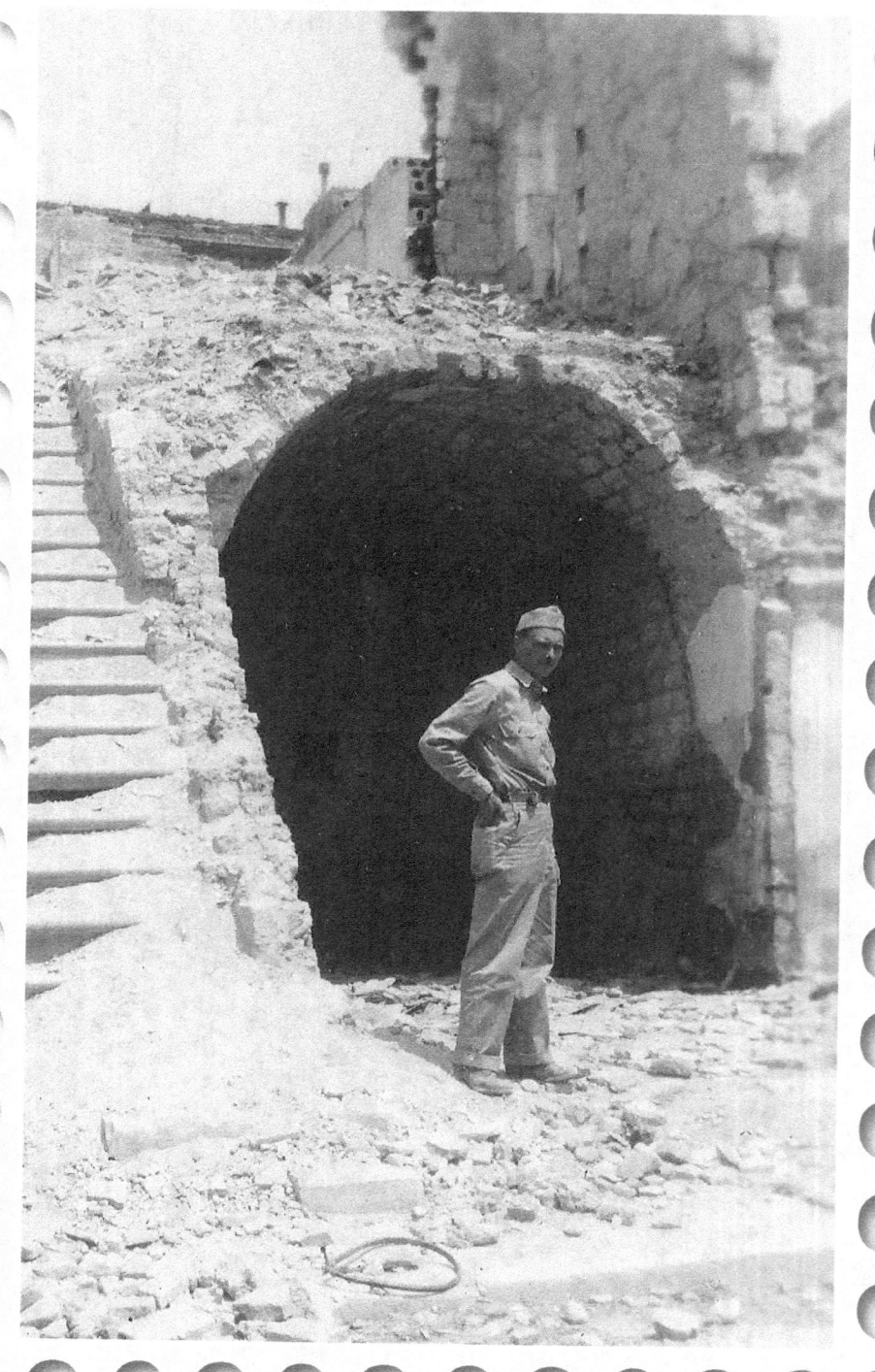

Rain would feel sweet
And wind and mud delitefull change—
A change from this—the walls,
These walls, the doors imprisoning;
Dim lite, harsh voices,
Reeking air from human breath,
Confined within these doors.

Is this a springtime?
Is there a rain-like mist on leaves?
And daffodils still blooming, yellow and tender,
Along the hedges, bordering trails?
Is there a canyon filled with fragrance,
With breezes steeped with music,
Restless with songs of freedom?

This: a Spring! But no—
If this be Spring, then where am I?
If this a year where Spring is not?
If Spring lies not asleep
Then it is I yet sleeping;
Please do waken me again—
When Spring is come.

Jesse LaVerd
Camp Kilmer, New Jersey

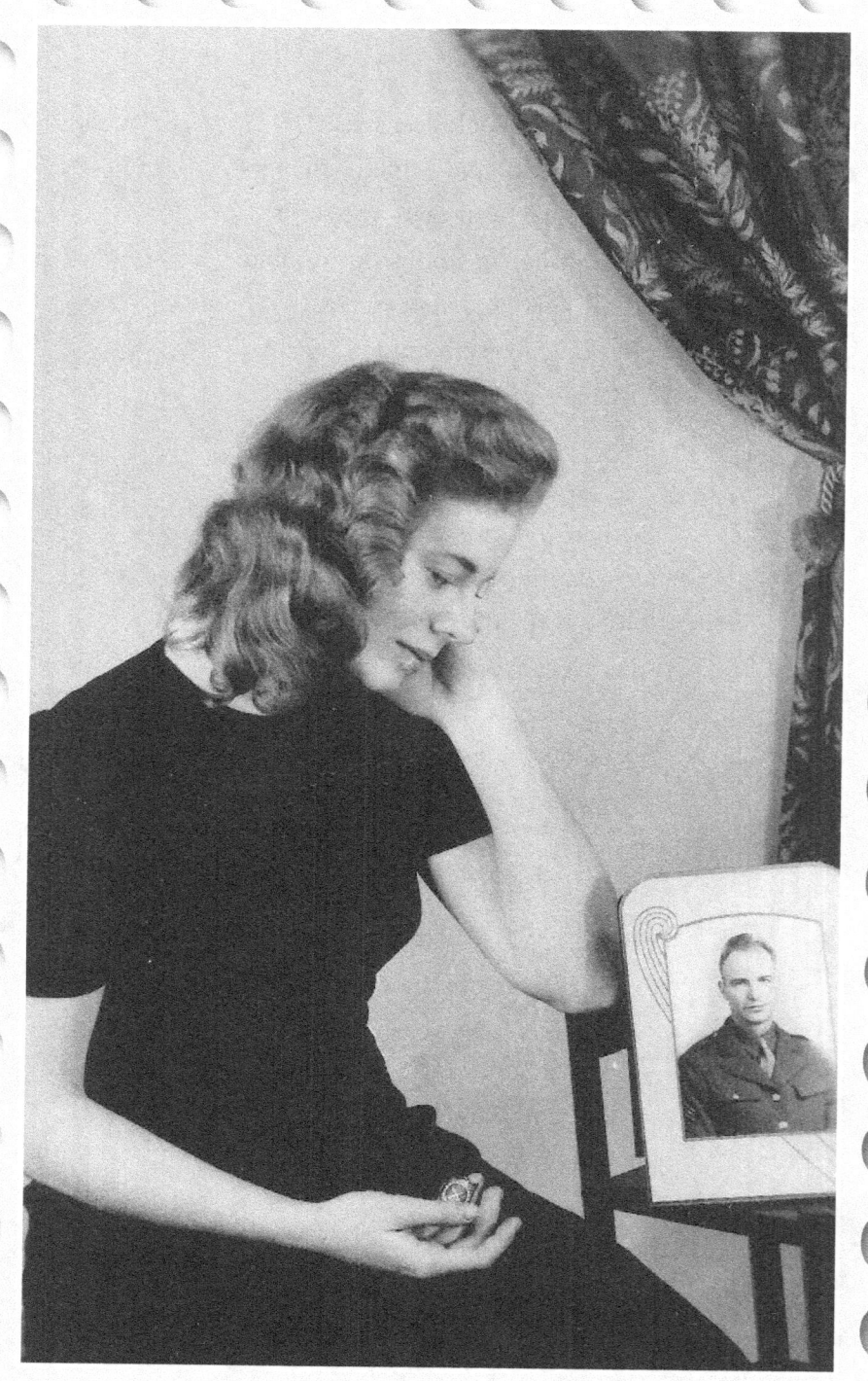

THE SOLDIER & HIS REDHEAD

Love Song

I envy the moon
Up there in the sky,
So high in the clouds
So fast gliding by—
My love.
I envy the moon
His free happy life,
The way he can travel
Alone every nite;
I know that he travels
Way over the sea—
He's watching over
My love.

Jesse LaVerd

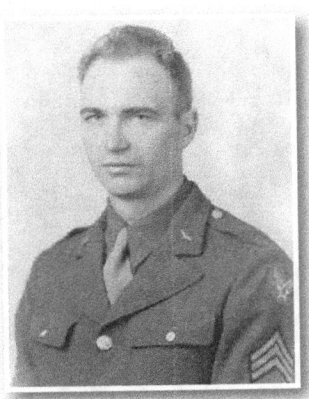

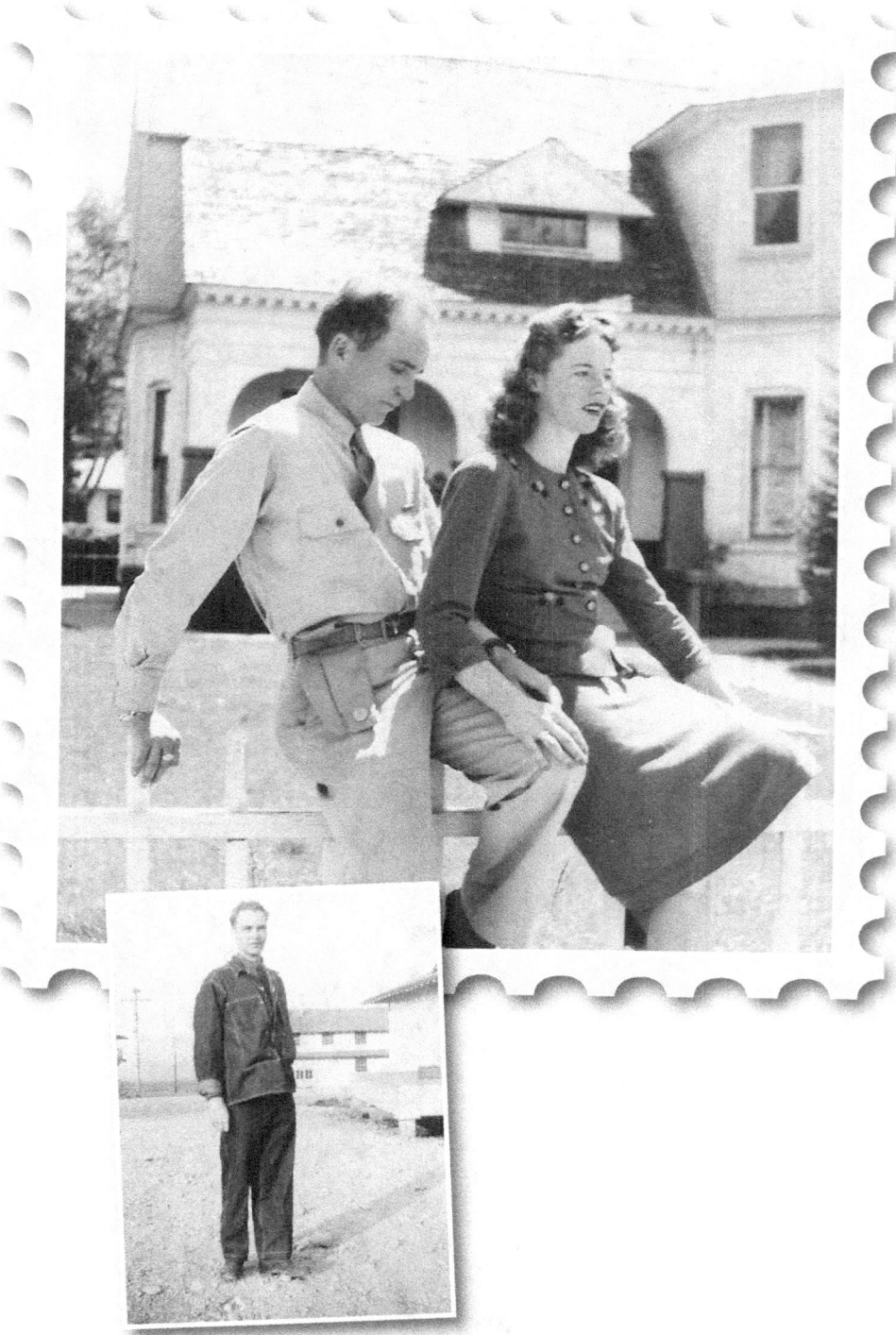

Sometime

Sometime I'm coming back to you,
Please don't fret or cry;
Sometime the bombs will cease to fall,
The warplanes cease to fly.

Sometime I'm going to leave this land
Of sun and sand and sky—
And then another life begins—
Someplace—for you and I.

Sometime—sometime I'm coming home,
Not yet, but bye and bye;
Until "our sometime" comes along,
Please pray, Sweetheart, don't cry.

Jesse LaVerd

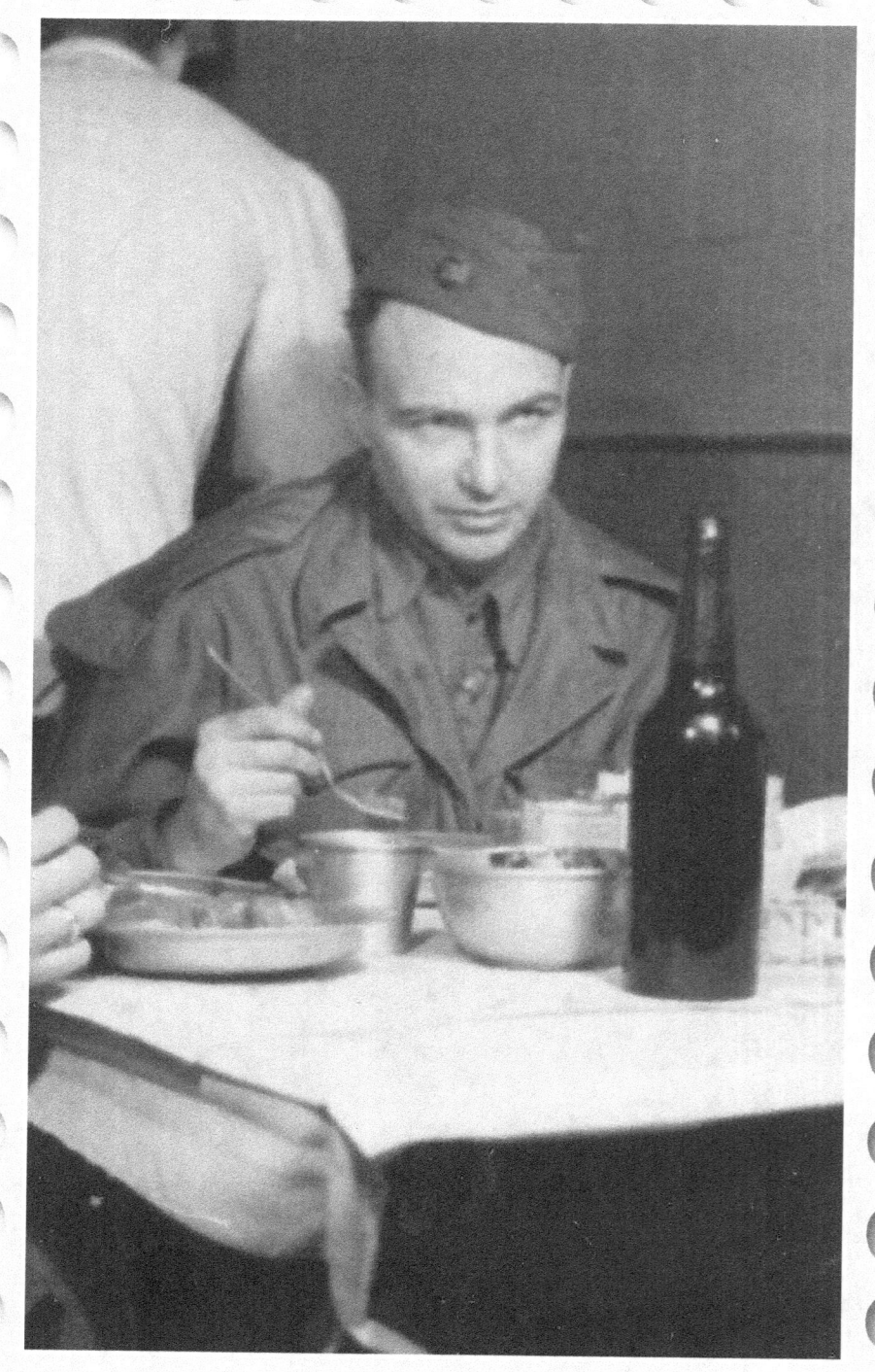

A Prayer for Christmas Eve, 1941

It snowed tonight, the myriad points of grey
Suspending in the air, then drifting down
To cover marks of steel and bomb.
High overhead, the moon rides by
On clouds of silver-grey and shades dark
And shunning scenes below of blood and war.

Below the pointed streak of searchlights' glare,
The snow-covered roofs of huddled barracks rise
While underneath, a frosty gleam of yellow light
Escapes the darkened window pane.
A Christmas tree adorned by mellow light
Casts softened gleams against the barrack walls
And soldiers' faces hard and grim.

God, let us know on battle fronts tonight
Where swirling flakes have settled down
On cannon grim, on warplanes sleek,
And, too, on tanks and stiffened forms within,
Let us know that Thou are still a God of Love and Right.

(Continues)

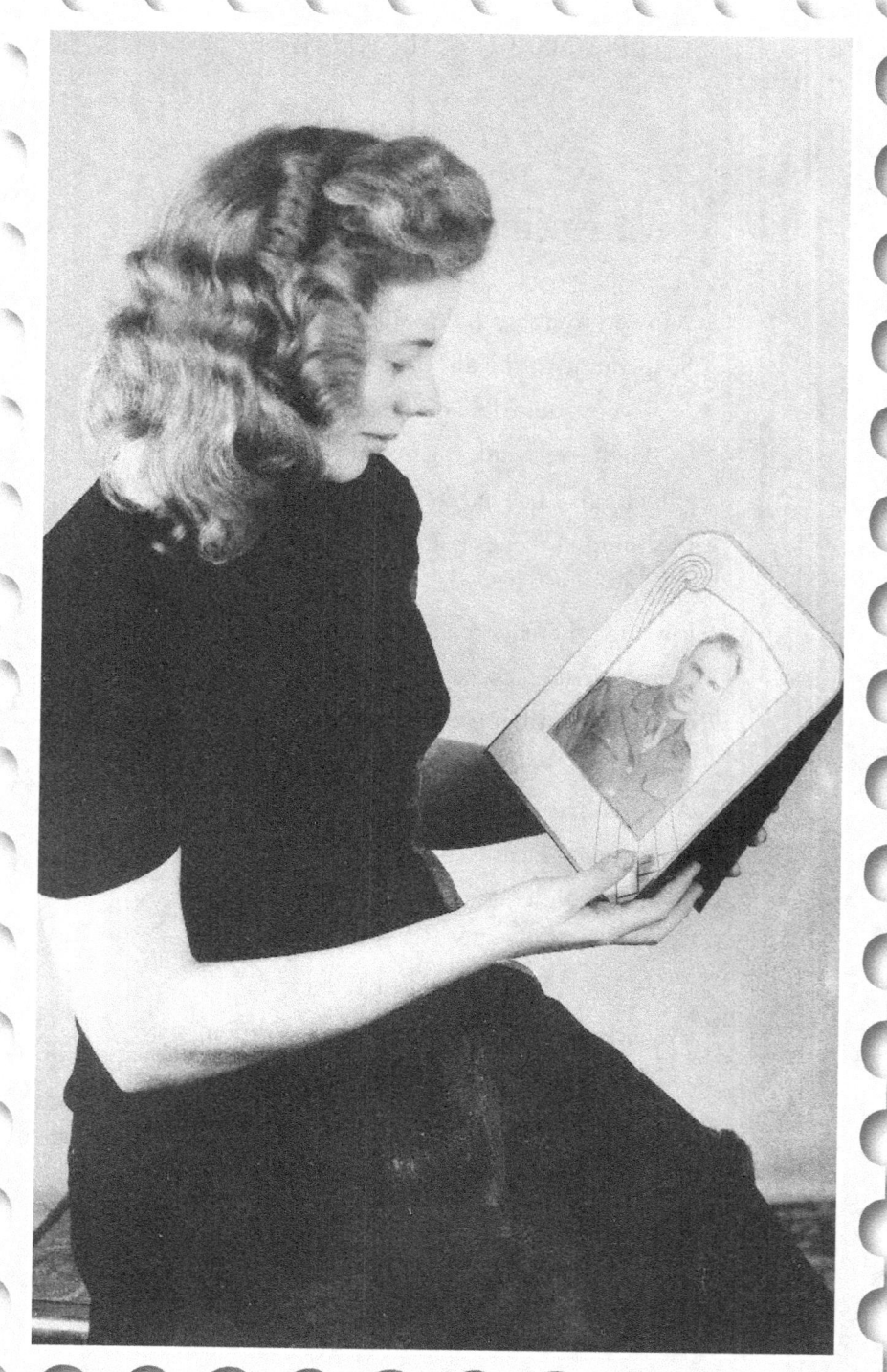

'Ay, let not the fear nor hatred of the foe
Becloud our minds from thoughts of love and home,
Where lonely hearts are praying, waiting our return;
That we may think of Christmas Eve, and too, of Him,

Whose birth we still remember.
God, we know that 'ere another Christmas comes—
Where two of us are now to carry on
But one will then remain. And unknown graves
And frozen shapes and blasted fragments strewn around
Will tell the endless tale of war and hate;
Ay, we know the dreary way.
But give us hope, and let us still remember happy days
And give us faith for days to come.

So let it snow tonight, and storm, and hail,
And when the storm of battle clears, help us
That we may not remember—and yet, may not forget—
This Christmas.

Jesse LaVerd

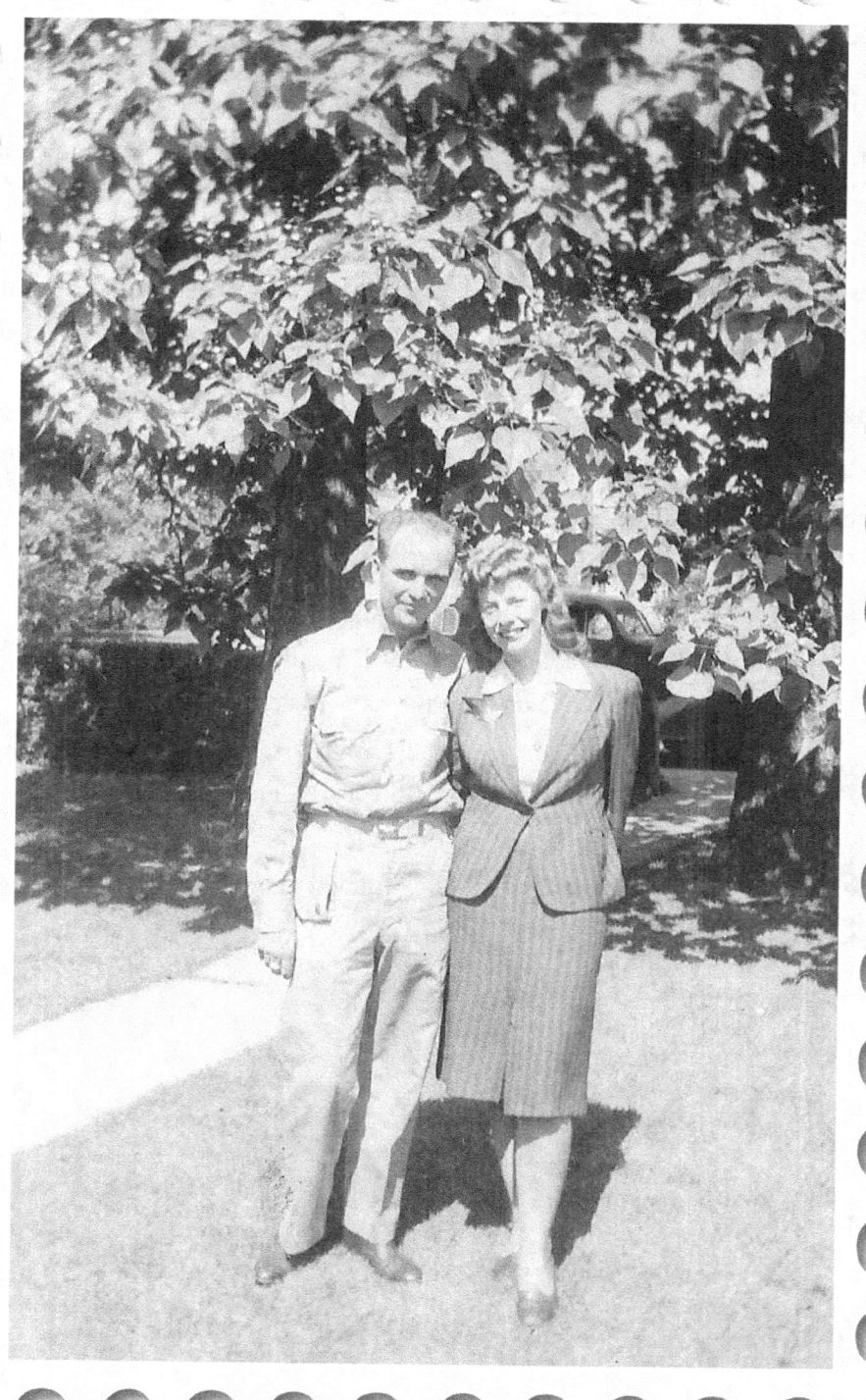

THE SOLDIER & HIS REDHEAD

To Flora

It is something wonderful to remember,
but it is more than recall and reminiscence,
more than knowing and feeing,
it is the realness of life, forever becoming new.

It includes dreams, prayers, and the longed-for,
but remains tenderly the same
when hopes and dreams are temporarily
obscured by problems of our every day.

It includes the meaningful part of all the beautiful
and lovely and wondrous things that are,
but when not expressed, the assurance remains
and there is no rejection.

It is expressed inadequately and, perchance,
only seldom, but the meaning thereof,
being of the heart and the spirit,
remains constant, even though unsaid.

(Continues)

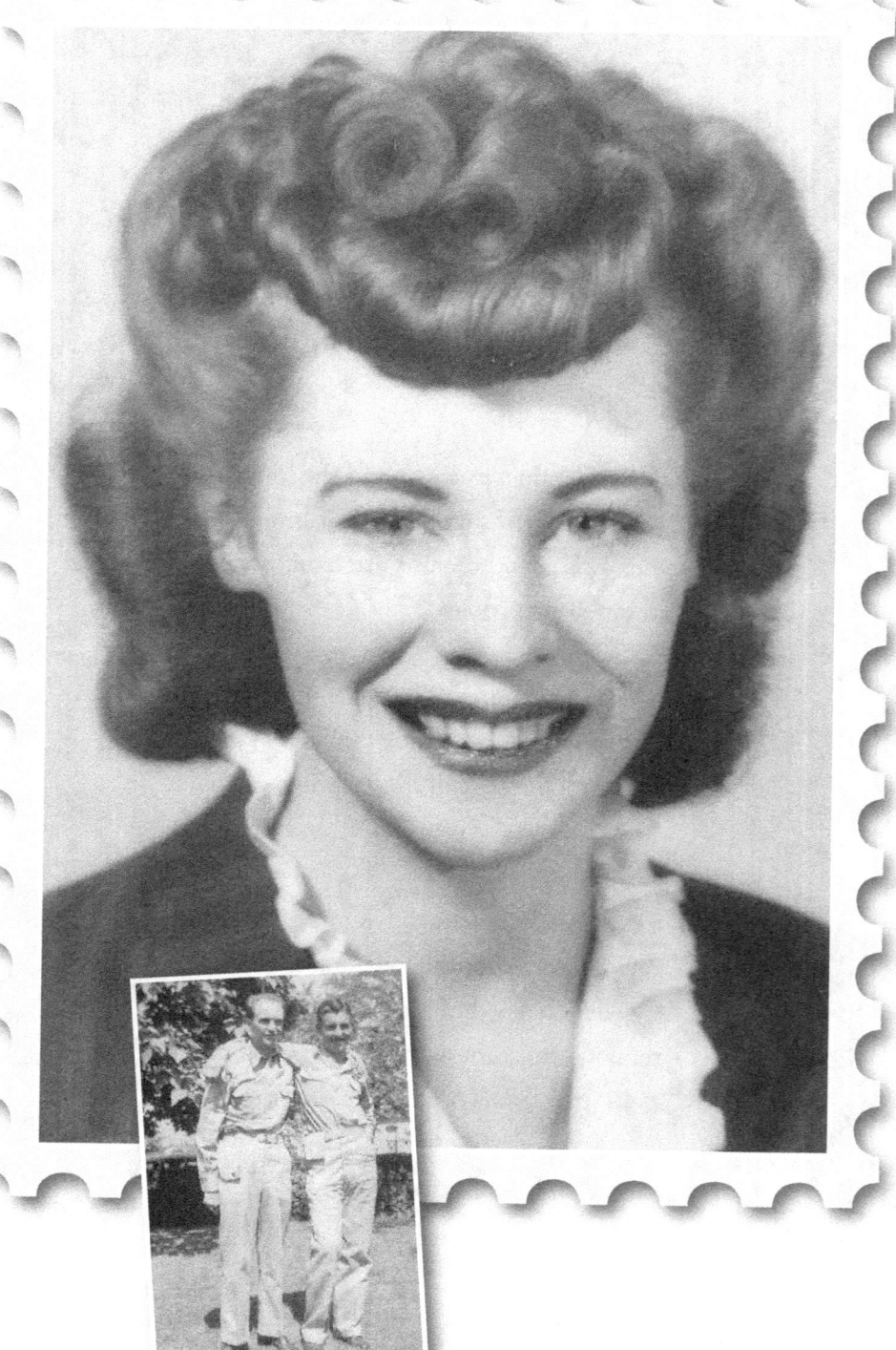

It is selfish in its demands,
expecting all and returning only meagerly,
but all remembrances and kindnesses
are cherished with tender gratitude.

It is something more than and beyond
daily problems, disappointments, and delights.
It is remembering the touch of your hands,
the shape of your face, the feel of your hair.

It is remembering you.
It is the playing of light and shadow
on tingling limbs, but it is more
than possessive lips and yielding flesh.

It is the mingling of sweetest emotions,
but it is more than seeing,
and touching and speaking.
It is knowing the loveliness of you.

It is most tender, but of all realities
it gives greatest strength meaning, and humbleness.
It is fiercely proud, but the pride is of the heart,
not of the mind, and newly-awakened feelings
of self-realization are expressed in reverential adoration.
It is all of this, and yet—it is more, so much more!

(Continues)

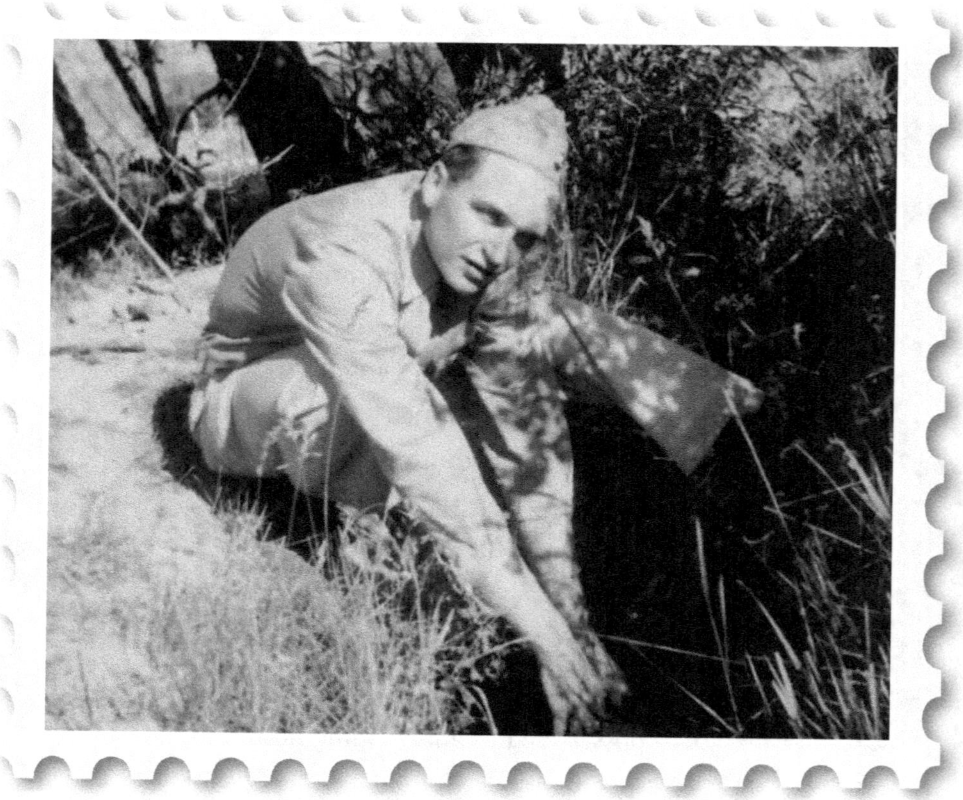

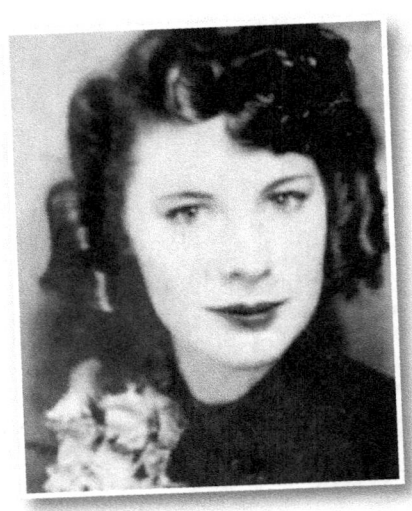
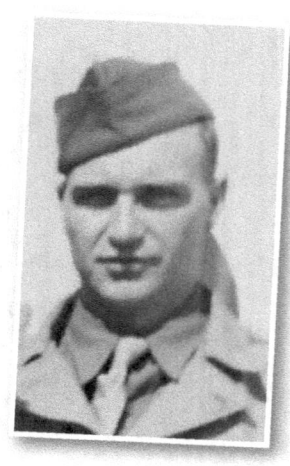

It is more than knowledge and appreciation
and beautiful memory.
It is experiencing these things day by day,
with hope and anticipation
claiming existence independent
of any present circumstance.

It is the past in memory,
the ever-present in realization,
the future in promise.
A continuous intertwining
of happiness and sadness.
it is remembered with wistful,
treasured with thankfulness,
anticipated with faith and assurance.

It is all that can be obtained,
all that may be desired,
all that can be fulfilled.
It is forever knowing
that someone loves you.

Jesse LaVerd

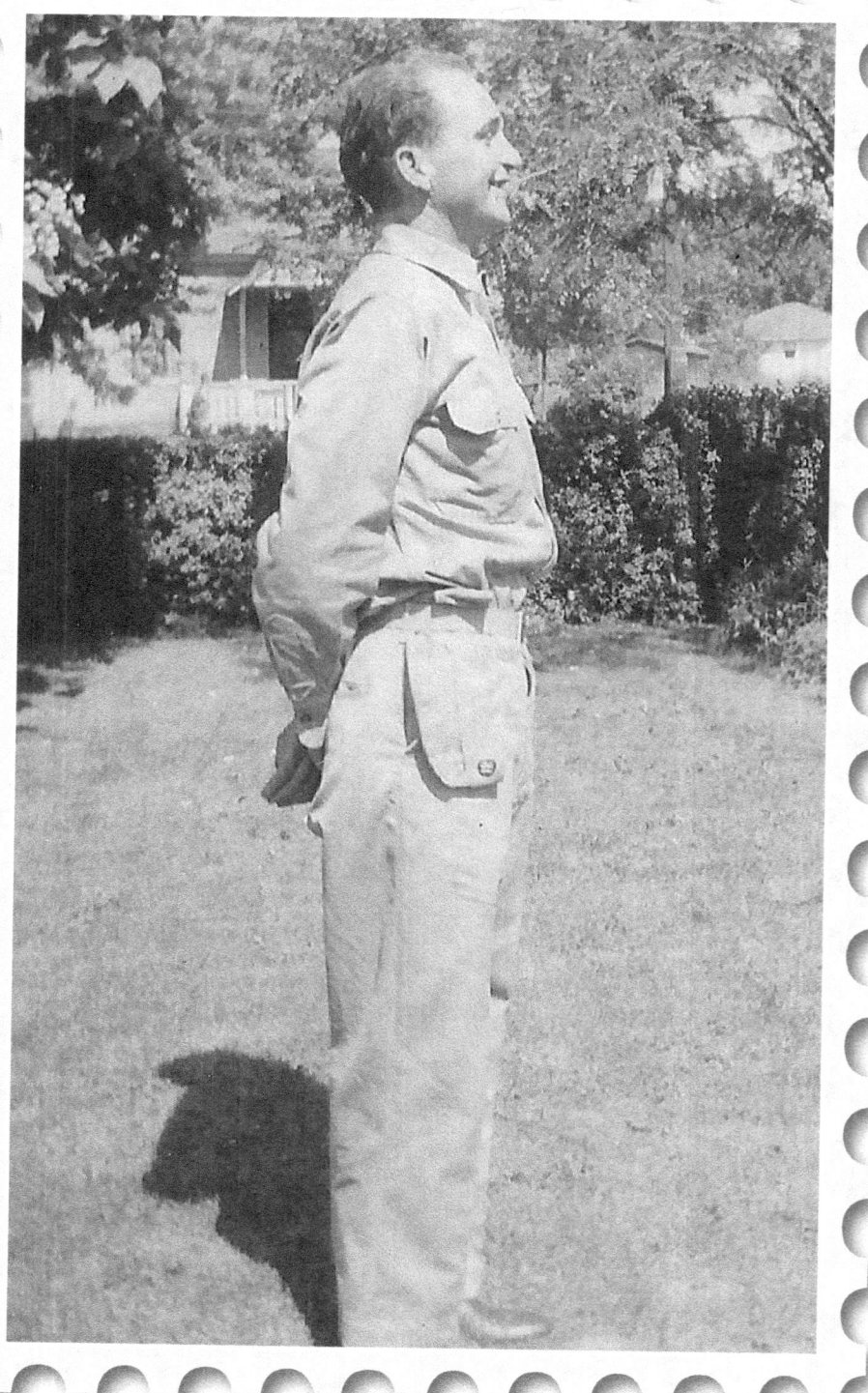

THE SOLDIER & HIS REDHEAD

My Wonderful One

You gave me a bit o' laughin'
A bit o' work and play
You gave me a bit o' carin'
To be sharin' day by day.
Just a little bit o' sunshine
A bit o' heaven, too.
And then to make it perfect
You just gave me you.

From the luckiest girl in all the world,
Flora

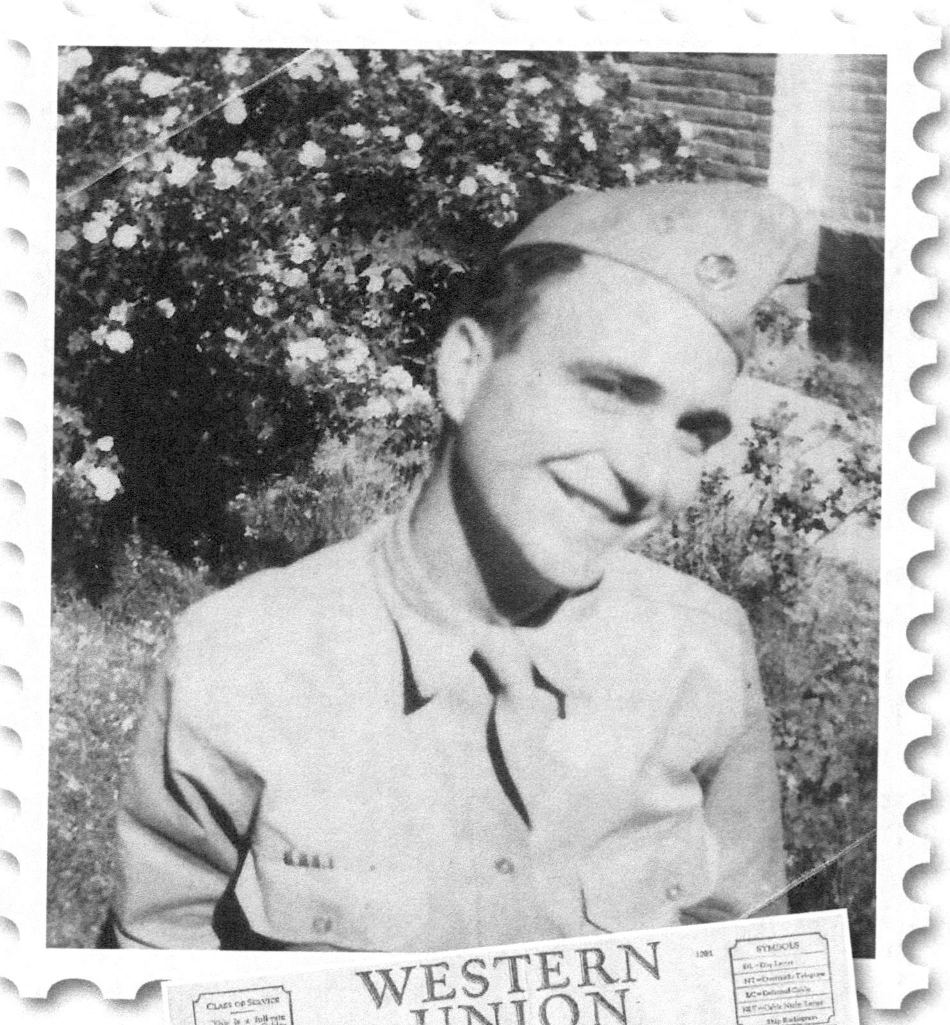

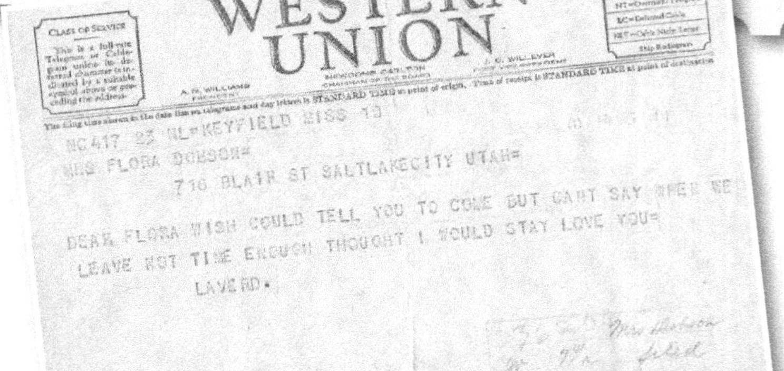

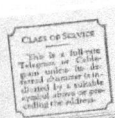

WESTERN UNION

NC417 23 NL=KEYFIELD MISS 13

MRS FLORA DOBSON=
716 BLAIR ST SALTLAKECITY UTAH=

DEAR FLORA WISH COULD TELL YOU TO COME BUT CANT SAY WHEN WE LEAVE NOT TIME ENOUGH THOUGHT I WOULD STAY LOVE YOU=

LAVERD.

SG LAVERD PERCY.

Christmas Eve

Tonight, my Darling
Think of me
Blue lights and silver
A sparkling Christmas tree.
It's needles heavy laden
With icicles and plastic snow
Sprinkled on these scented branches
My Darling, don't you know
The flames in the fire place
Are burning low.

I'm living a dream here with you
But it's soon tomorrow.
True—stockings are full
The tree a delight,
Our star you placed with such care
But fleecy whiteness piles into the night
And two weary heads must find rest.
Our pillow is waiting
So off with the slippers
I love you, LaVerd, my Darling
—Goodnight—

Flora

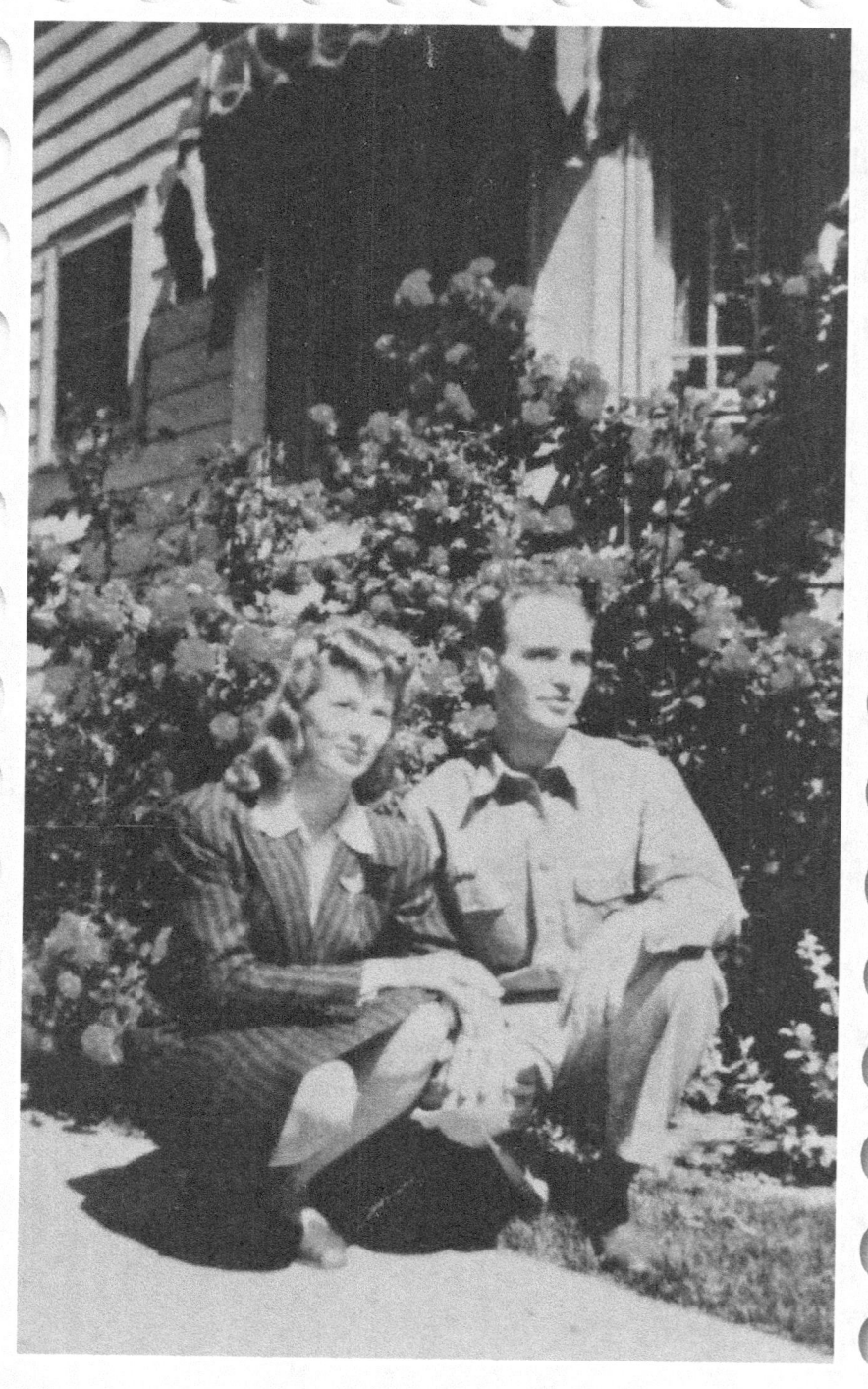

A Soldier Dreams

My cares, my fears
I cast them all
away, to join my dreams.

Jesse LaVerd

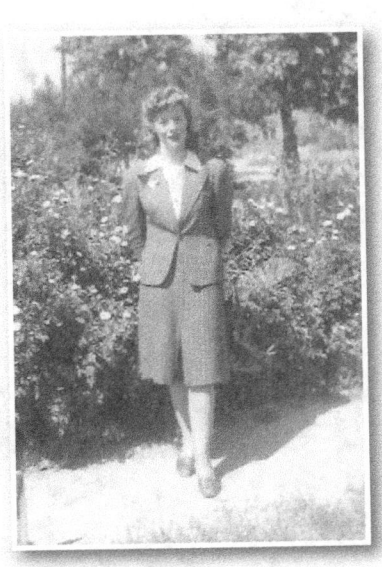

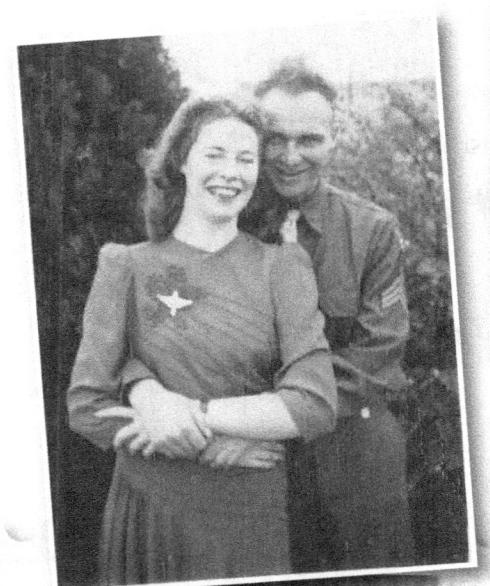
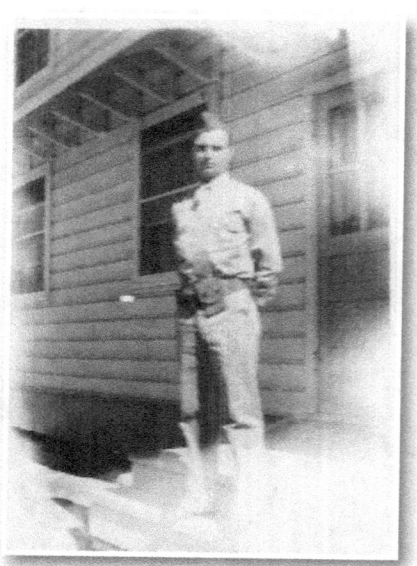
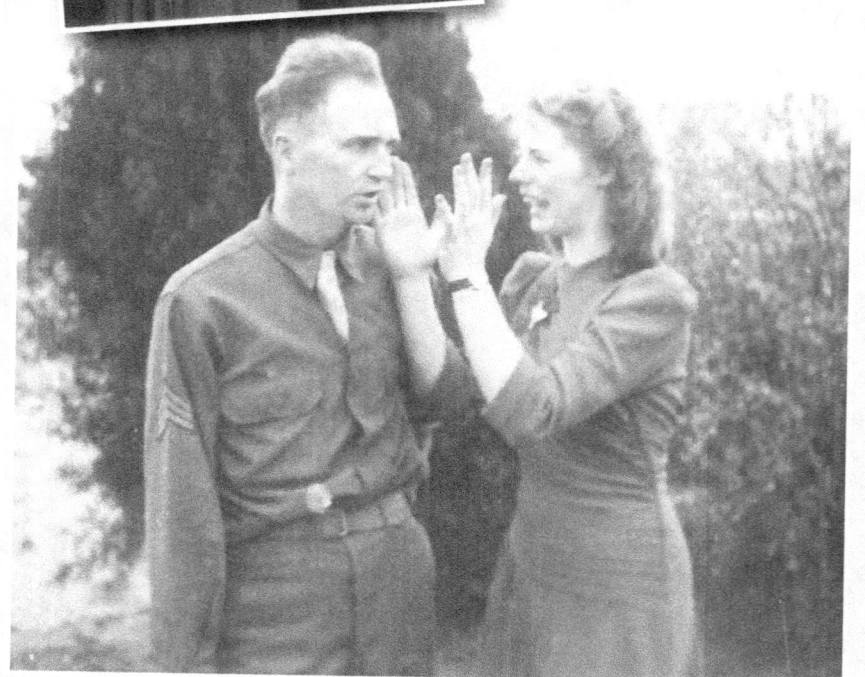

The Hours

On our Easter Day
We found Spring—you and I
And then
Said once again
—Goodbye.

Jesse LaVerd

The Days

I have an Easter containing three days,
Of six wondrous hours with you.
We saw the "Bug Town."
Spoke with one of renown,
Then were lost in the multitude.

Flora

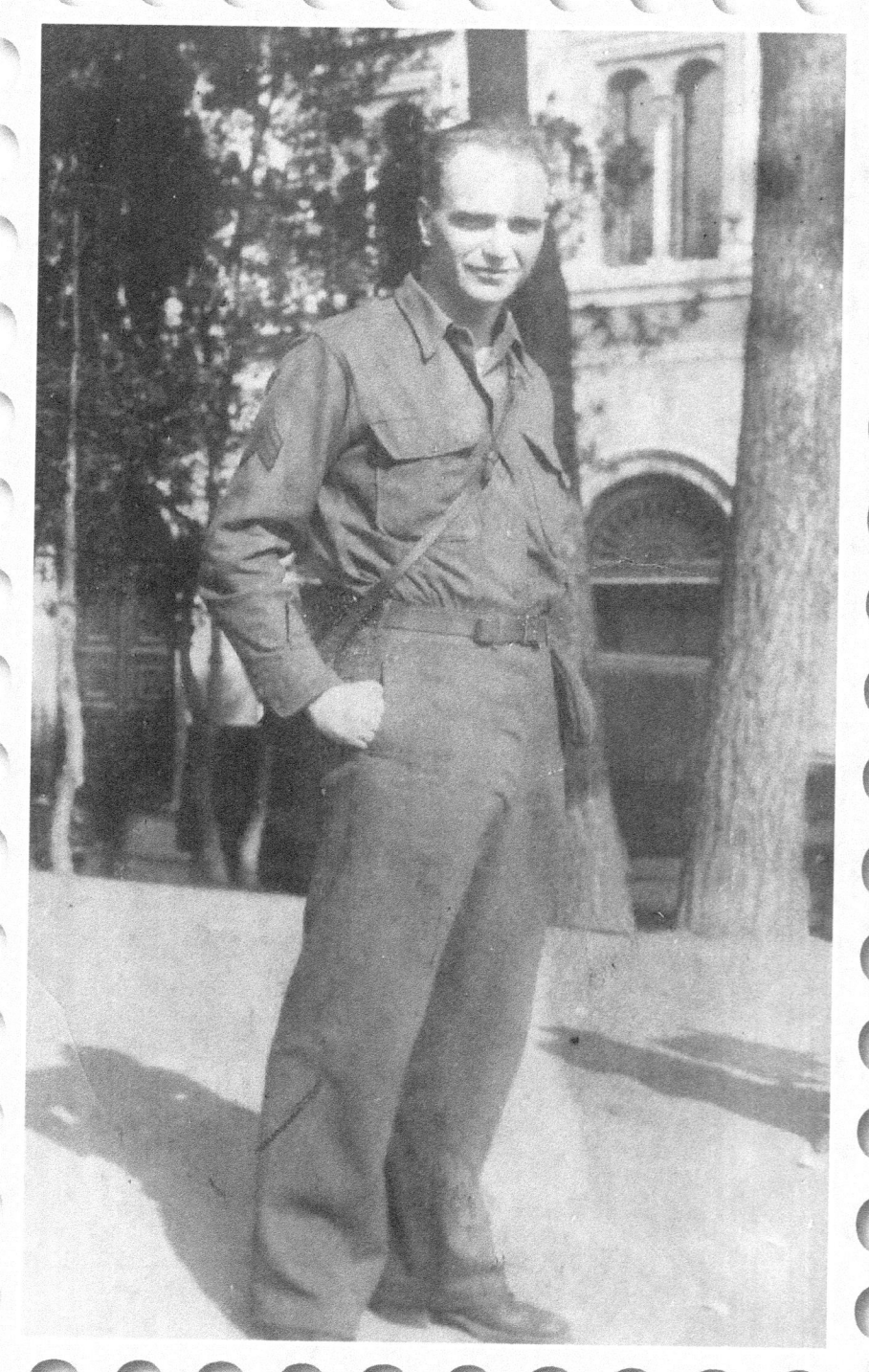

My Dreams are Mine

My dreams are mine;
I cannot share with coming nite
Of flitting shadows, stars and sand,
Nor give them to the desert breeze
To drift across the world.

My dreams are mine:
I will not give them to the rain
To shower down on rocks and hills,
Nor breathe them to a golden sky
When day is done.

These dreams of mine—
I shall not lose on foreign shores.
But when once more I touch your hand
I'll share my dreams
And dream new dreams with you.

Jesse LaVerd

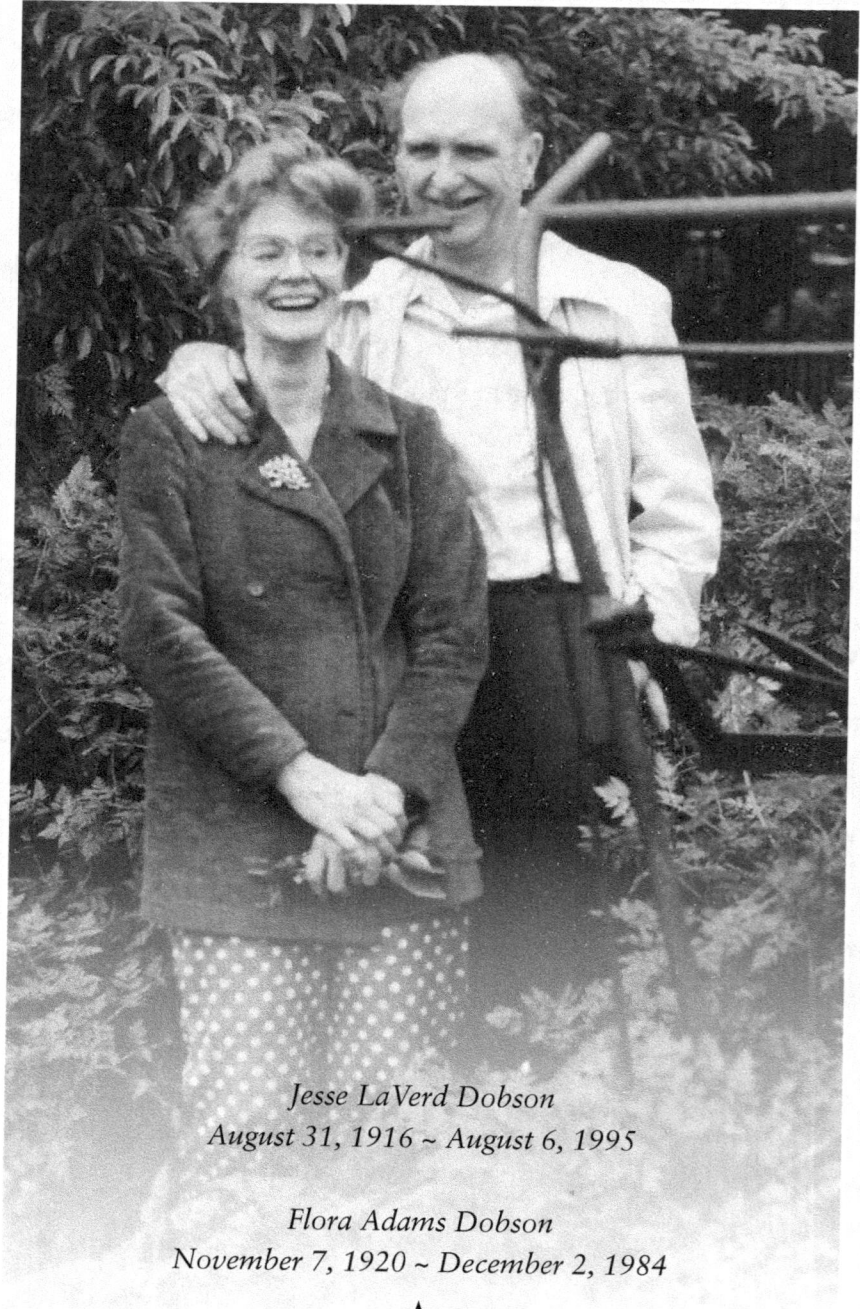

Jesse LaVerd Dobson
August 31, 1916 ~ August 6, 1995

Flora Adams Dobson
November 7, 1920 ~ December 2, 1984

Ducks

In our backyard are three tame ducks
Dabbling around in the hay and muck,
Intent on getting their share and more
Of the over-flowing barnyard store.

Fat and lazy with useless wings,
Quacking and poking around in things.
But they sometimes see wild ducks go by
In feathered flight across the sky
And flap their wings, and try to fly.

Now I think my soul's like a tame old duck
Dabbling around—not expecting much.
But sometimes when the north wind sings
And howls and moans and when if flings
The wild things hurtling overhead—
My soul recalls something lost and dead.

It remembers a time now long gone by
When it would dream and soar and fly;
Now it's fairly content with the shape it's in—
But it's not the old duck that it might have been!

Jesse LaVerd

OUR STAR

I have seen our star
White and glowing,
Shimmering in the desert nile,
Or paled by moonbeams
Then lost among the clouds.

I have watched our star
Blue-white, shining down
Upon this sand and sea
Bidding radiance be subdued
When vanishing in water,
Dropping from the sky.

I have sent our star
A message long and sweet,
A song, a word of love,
A hope, an inspiration,
All this, and more — ah,
So much more! — have I sent
Upward and skyward to our star
To give you dreams.

I have seen our star
White and glowing,
And with its stardust
I have sent my love to you.

North Africa
August 1943

www.ingramcontent.com/pod-product-compliance
Lightning Source LLC
Chambersburg PA
CBHW070318220526
45465CB00004B/1905